Dawlish 1985.
G.W.R. 150 yrs.

Ray Keith

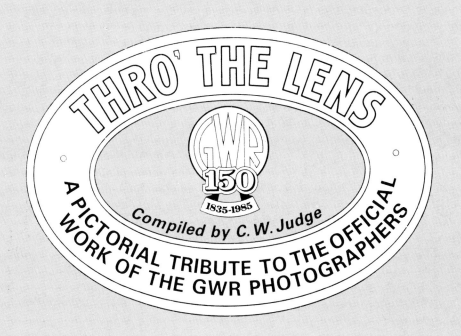

THRO' THE LENS

GWR
150
1835-1985

A PICTORIAL TRIBUTE TO THE OFFICIAL WORK OF THE GWR PHOTOGRAPHERS

Compiled by C. W. Judge

THE BRISTOL BATH & LONDON WAGON.
THE FORERUNNER OF THE G.W.R. GOODS TRAIN.

Plate 1: The power and majesty of a Great Western 'Castle' class 4-6-0, No. 4078 *Pembroke Castle*. The unreality of this huge engine running and working hard at high speed but remaining stationary on the test plant in Swindon Works is well captured in this picture. The plant, built in 1904, had five sets of rollers, four sets being braked, and all were capable of being moved to match the wheel centres of the locomotive on test. Speeds of up to 80m.p.h. were attained and the braking was carried out by water-cooled hydraulic brakes. This was another first for the Great Western Railway, as this type of engine testing had only previously been carried out by test-hauling a train.

THRO' THE LENS

GWR 150 1835-1985

Compiled by C. W. Judge

A PICTORIAL TRIBUTE TO THE OFFICIAL WORK OF THE GWR PHOTOGRAPHERS

DOMINE · DIRIGE · NOS   VIRTUTE · ET · INDUSTRIA

COAT OF ARMS OF THE GREAT WESTERN RAILWAY
CO. BEING A BLENDING OF THE ARMS OF THE CITIES
OF LONDON AND BRISTOL — THE ORIGINAL LIMITS
OF THE GREAT WESTERN RAILWAY AS
CONTEMPLATED BY THE G.W.R. ACT OF 1835.

Published by

OPC railprint

A JOINT VENTURE BETWEEN BRITISH RAIL AND OXFORD PUBLISHING CO.

ISBN 0-86093-312-1 (hbk)
     86093-356-3 (pbk)

Typesetting by:
Aquarius Typesetting Services, New Milton, Hants.

Printed in Great Britain by:
Biddles Ltd., Guildford and Kings Lynn

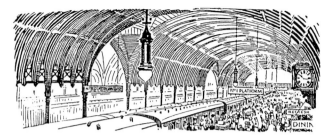

All the pen and ink sketches are reproductions from original Great Western Railway Publications.

Plate 2: Before the invention of the camera, the railway scenes and events were recorded by the engravers of the time, and this particular view by the famous Bourne shows broad gauge tracks and bridges at Wootton Bassett, with a policeman in charge of the point switch and capstan signal.

Published by:
Railprint
Oxford Publishing Co.
Link House
West Street
POOLE, Dorset

Railprint is a joint venture between British Rail and Oxford Publishing Co.

Acknowledgements

My kindest thanks go to Chris Potts for advising and checking the manuscript, to Ian Kennedy for help in 'finding' the photographs, to R. W. Drummond, British Rail, Western Region, for his co-operation in compiling the book, and finally to Sue for deciphering the captions for typing.

Introduction

As 1985 marks the 150th anniversary of the Great Western Railway and Western Region of British Rail, it seemed fitting to pay tribute to the work of the official photographers of this great railway.

Although many of the pictures in the photographic collection have been used within the numerous books on the GWR over the years, no tribute to this small band of company photographers, who skillfully portrayed the day to day working and activities of the Great Western Railway, has previously been published. This book then attempts to capture many of the varied duties these men were required to carry out over the entire system, up to 1947 and nationalisation. When it is realised that, in the early 1880s, their equipment consisted of 12in. x 10in. cameras, made in brass and mahogany, enormous tripods and heavy 12in. x 10in. glass photographic plates, one can understand why early photographs of the GWR are not numerous — visualise the walk along Sonning Cutting or Dawlish sea wall with such equipment!

The turn of the century, and up to the early 1920s was mainly contained on these large negatives, but after this date, 8in. x 6in. and 7in. x 5in. negatives were used which allowed more flexibility of equipment resulting in a larger number of pictures being taken on location.

When selecting the contents for this book, I asked 'why' was the picture taken? The answer was not always forthcoming, as sometimes even the official registers did not reveal the secret! In these cases I have had to set out my own views on the reason for the photograph. The selection, is, I hope, as varied and comprehensive as possible, within the pages available, from such a large collection. I have avoided using, wherever possible, photographs seen before, but in a minority of subjects, only a few photographs are available and these therefore have to be reused.

Remembering the famous GWR phrase, this book is designed to appeal to 'boys (and girls) of all ages' and will, I hope, remind those who knew the Company, and inform those who did not, of the wonderful years of 'The Great Western Railway'. Without the 'official photographer', the reader would be poorer by far and our knowledge of the system much reduced. As someone once said, 'one good photograph is worth a thousand words'.

Colin Judge
March 1985

Contents

The Broad and Mixed Gauge

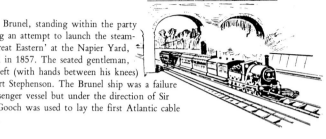

Plate 3 : Brunel, standing within the party watching an attempt to launch the steamship 'Great Eastern' at the Napier Yard, Millwall in 1857. The seated gentleman, on the left (with hands between his knees) is Robert Stephenson. The Brunel ship was a failure as a passenger vessel but under the direction of Sir Daniel Gooch was used to lay the first Atlantic cable in 1866.

Plate 4 (below): The conversion of the gauge began at daybreak on Saturday, 21st May 1892 in fine weather conditions. All the new points and crossings were already on site and the ballast had been removed from between the rail. Each alternate transom had also been cut. The actual operation consisted of removing the fixing bolts and tie rods, and cutting the remaining transoms to standard gauge width. The second stage was to slew the track inwards, seen in the accompanying view, and then finally refix bolts and rods before reballasting. The 177 miles between Exeter and Penzance was 'narrowed' in two days with standard gauge trains running again on Monday, 23rd May 1892. A remarkable feat of engineering.

GREAT WESTERN RAILWAY
BROAD-GAUGE ENGINE
"Great Britain,"
Which accomplished the fastest journey on record- viz : from Paddington to Didcot 53¼ miles in 47 minutes.

The Train was the 9-15 Express to Bristol, and consisted of Four Carriages and Van, and was driven on May 11th, 1848, by

J. MICHAEL ALMOND, Driver.
RICHARD DENHAM, Fireman.

Plate 5: The broad gauge in South Wales. Llansamlet Station (near Swansea) from an official photograph taken in 1868 showing the early type of 'Board' or 'Fantail' signal and capstan for point operation, with the operator at his post.

Sir Daniel Gooch elected chairman of the GWR in 1865; also M.P. for Swindon

Plates 6a & 6b: This series of photographs was taken in May 1892 when the Great Western Railway was quadrupling the main line between Didcot and Taplow during 1892/3 (except for the mile and a half through Reading Yard which was not complete until 1899). Various small lengths were opened in 1892 but the main part opened in 1893. The new tracks were added either on the north or south of the existing tracks, and in one case, in Sonning Cutting, either side *(Plate 6a)*. The second view *(Plate 6b)* shows Cherry Lane Bridge (occupation bridge) just having been demolished, with considerable interest from the local inhabitants, including a small girl on the track. Note how the track has been crudely protected by large wooden beams.

Plate 7: This view shows two of the contractor's locomotives (with dog) hauling in the girders for the new 'four track' bridge.

Plate 9 (right upper): The jovial band of inspectors and officials, photographed in May 1892, are obviously pleased with their results.

Plates 10 & 11a (right lower): The two final views in this series were photographed on 16th May 1892 and show, firstly, the 2.35p.m. 'down' express with a standard gauge train and, secondly, for comparison, a broad gauge express at 10.15a.m. on the same day. The location is at the east end of Maidenhead Station and includes the slotted post signals about to be replaced. The slotted post signal originally showed 'danger' when the arm was horizontal, 'all clear' when the arm was out of sight within the post, and 'caution' when in the half-way position (but this was changed to the 'all clear' indication in 1871).

Plate 8: This tells the present day reader a great deal about the engineering feats of the last century. The mammoth upright square post, with its block and pulley, makes one wonder how much man/horse power was necessary to raise this huge girder. This photograph also shows well the mixed gauge track and slotted post signal alongside the signal box.

Plate 11b (right): This is a facsimile of a letter of thanks (dated 1st September 1892), to the staff who carried out the conversion of the gauge, signed by G. K. Mills who was Secretary to the GWR from May 1892 to June 1910.

Great Western Railway,

London Terminus.
Paddington. W.

1st September 1892.

Dear Sir,

In receiving the report of the carrying
out of the conversion of the Gauge on the
Co's Lines in the West of England in May
last, the Board expressed themselves as highly
gratified at the successful completion of the
operation and at the hearty manner in
which every member of the Staff engaged
in it had performed his share of the work.

Thinking it may be of interest to you, I
have the pleasure to send you the accompanying
copy of the minute which was passed by
the Directors on the occasion.

Yours faithfully,

G.K. Mills

Mr A Lewis.

Brunel Bridges

Plate 12 (left): With the 10.50p.m. Falmouth to Truro train passing over the Collegewood Viaduct near Penryn, on Saturday 21st July 1934, came the end of the famous Brunel timber structures. Having stood the stresses of heavy loading for over 50 years, the 42 timber viaducts between Plymouth and Falmouth spanned a total length of 4.8 miles, with a further ten viaducts between Truro and Penzance spanning a further 1.03 miles. All these timber viaducts were replaced by masonry structures and this picture shows Keyham Viaduct, just outside Plymouth, under reconstruction in 1899, as a prelude to doubling of the line at this point. The supports nearest the camera are marked '2/83' and I think it fair to assume these were installed in February 1883.

Plate 13 (right): This picture of the building of the 201yd. masonry viaduct at Coombe, near Saltash, in 1894 includes the old timber Brunel viaduct it replaced and the famous Brunel Saltash Bridge featured in the background, thus this scene shows three GWR bridge structures in one photograph.

Plate 14 (above): This view shows the beautiful curve of the old Collegewood Viaduct which was the last timber viaduct (974ft. in length) in the West Country to be replaced by a masonry structure. This photograph was taken in 1932 (prior to reconstruction), from the north side looking towards Falmouth.

Plate 15 (right): A new Forder Viaduct, near Saltash, seen under construction in October 1906, as part of the deviation inland between Wearde and St. Germans which enabled five viaducts to be replaced by only three. The variety of engineering skills used to build such a bridge can be clearly seen in this interesting view.

Locomotive Running Sheds

Plate 16: Didcot locomotive shed, pictured when new in 1932, and photographed from the side of the coaling plant. The new four-road building was 210ft. long by 67ft. wide, and could hold up to sixteen engines. This project was undertaken by the Great Western Railway under a Government-sponsored loan scheme. Also included in the new facility were the lifting shop (with 50 ton hoist), coal stage with overhead water tank, boiler washing facilities, and a plant for calcinating sand. This is now the home of the Great Western Society whose magnificent efforts have helped to keep the GWR alive today!

Plate 17 (above): Whenever anything new was produced or alterations made, the Great Westrn photographer was called in 'for the record'. This view shows the new 65ft. turntable installed at Oxford in 1906 and was one of fifteen previously authorised by the Directors. They were all to a 'standard' drawing and were known as the 'overgirder' or 'surface' type. This type did not require a deep pit, and the working parts were easy to service. The engine on the turntable is one of the 'Queen' class, No. 1125, which, incidentally, was withdrawn from service in the same year.

Plate 19: Fishguard Shed was a standard Church-ward shed, offering the usual facilities. The coaling stage was somewhat different, with a non-standard water tank and a corrugated lean-to type of wagon protection. This photograph was taken to show the alterations being carried out on the coaling stage.

Plate 20: The Great Western appeared to take a series of locomotive shed photographs in the 1920s and this one, in May 1926, shows Duffryn Yard with the old coaling stage; this was replaced in 1931. The yard also, at that time, had only five roads into the sheds, whereas in 1947, six were in use.

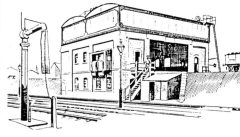

Plate 18 (left): A view of Old Oak Common shed coaling plant is shown here. This building was 104ft. by 59ft. 6in. and had four double and two single coal tips, and a 4-section water tank over the top holding over ¼ million gallons of water. This was a 'standard pattern' type building, and the largest on the system. The two centre roads for the coal wagons had a ramp incline of 1 in 50 up to the appliance, and 1 in 80 on the bank (supported unusually on brick arches). The complete running shed layout was the largest on the Great Western Railway, and many official photographs recorded fine views of this shed.

Plate 21 (right): Exeter Shed and yard, in 1921, with the coaling stage on the left and the locomotive shed on the right. The turntable position is shown in the centre with a tender engine 'blowing off' whilst awaiting turning. The variance between the MR, GNR, LNWR and GWR wagons makes them worthy of a second glance.

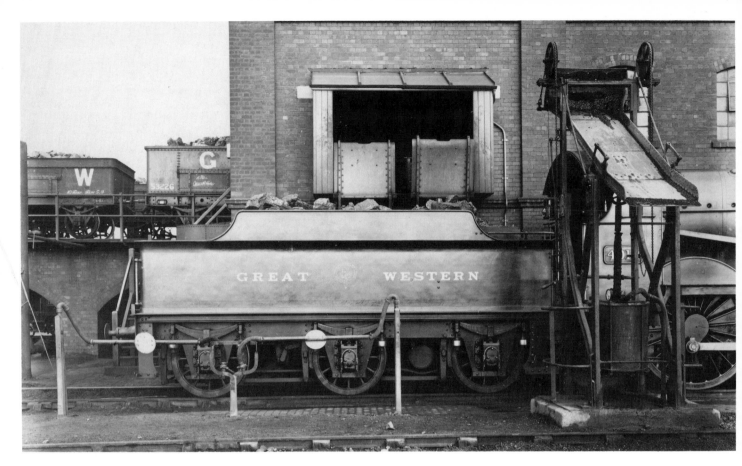

Plates 22 & 23: Inventions were plentiful within the life of the GWR, and the official photographer was always called upon to record these events. Here, at Old Oak Common, an engine steam-operated ash plant was installed and these two views show the siting of the equipment. At the time the picture was taken, it was to capture the details of the installation, but now it allows the reader to observe the many other fine features within the photograph, namely details of wagons, locomotive, livery and coaling stage construction.

Plate 24: This shows the wagon fitting room (machine portion) in the Wagon Department. The noise from the hundreds of slapping belts must have been considerable. The huge lamps are also interesting above this 'maze' of machinery.

Swindon Works

So much has been written about Swindon Works that the next series of pictures are included as a tribute not only to the famous Works, but also the talent of the official Swindon Works photographer. Nearly all these pictures were taken on heavy 12in. x 10in. glass plates (together with a very heavy mahogany camera), therefore the awkwardness of this type of equipment had to be overcome. Thank goodness that the resultant prints are so clear.

Plate 25 (left): This view portrays the 'X' Shop in Swindon Works, used to construct points and crossings. Upon the receipt of the Engineer's drawing, all the fittings were accurately set out on benches, and after drilling, bending, machining, etc. were fitted together, with a careful check on 'gauging'. The shop measured 240ft. by 180ft. and was fitted with overhead lifting appliances. The particular trackwork illustrated was for Cardiff in 1937.

Plate 26 (overleaf upper): When special crossings and larger crossings were required, these were often assembled outside, as seen in this view photographed in August 1935.

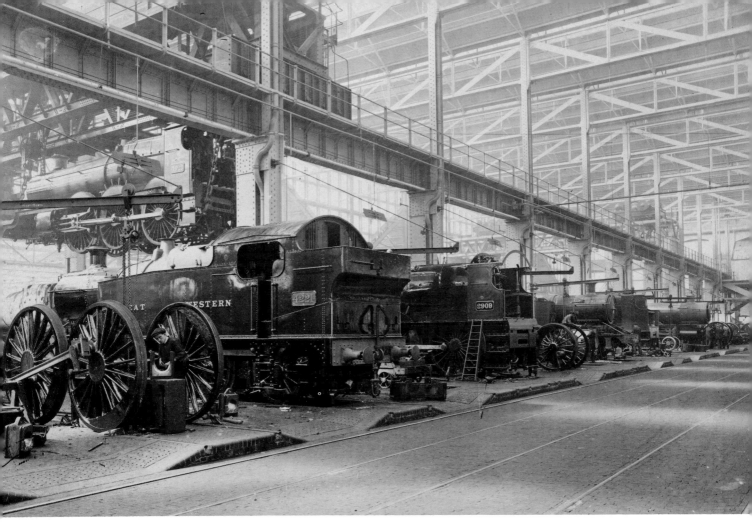

Plate 28: A superb view of the Erecting Shop ('AE') with the 100 ton crane in action, moving 'Star' class locomotive No. 4022 around the shop. The wheels in the left foreground are off one of the French Compounds which the GWR owned, and it is unusual to have the coupling rods attached as in this view.

Plate 29: The opening of a new Great Western laundry at Swindon, in April 1938, prompted the Works photographer to attend. This plant could deal with five and a quarter million items a year, and replaced an original laundry (built in 1893) in the Carriage Works. Many of the items such as towels, sheets from the hotels, serviettes, and all the other pieces from stations, etc., were brought in by the fleet of travelling stores vans for a fast and efficient service from the ladies of Swindon.

Entrance GWR Works, Swindon.

Plate 27 (left): The 'V' Shop was the Boiler Shop, and this photograph is the only one found in the collection showing an 'overfull' situation, with more than fifty boilers receiving attention. Perhaps this was the reason for the photograph on 15th November 1927. The noise of riveting must have been overwhelming especially for the small boy apprentices in the centre foreground of the picture.

Plate 30: The Carriage Paint Shop at Swindon, lit by another of the inverted incandescent gas lights, was probably the only place to see a GWR coach in 'mint' condition, before service conditions caused the paintwork to lose its sheen. The finish on the coaches seen in this view would have been applied as follows: red lead, filling, then stained and rubbed down, lead colour, ground colour, lake, and subsequently signwriting, lettering and the Company's crest applied. After lining by special machines, the whole of the coach was given four coats of varnish. The variety of stock in this view had again been arranged for the Works photographer and for a subsequent article in the *GWR Magazine*.

G.W.R. Mechanics' Institute

Plate 31 (above): 'The chemical laboratory and research section of the Chief Mechanical Engineer's Department', was the description of the location pictured here in 1916. This dealt with two aspects of the railway; namely 'safety and efficiency' and 'claims and rates'. Tests were carried out here on samples of most purchases made by the GWR as well as water, coal, etc. Investigation into insurance claims made on the Company also found their way here if a chemist's report was needed.

Plate 32: This is an unusual photograph as it shows a self-propelled 6 ton steam crane, with coupled wheels in use, in the late 1890s in Swindon Works' saw mill yard. Even this vehicle was fully lined out and had a copper-capped chimney in true Great Western style!

Plate 33: The 'A' shed, erected around 1841, and referred to in those days as the 'engine establishment'. It was 480ft. long by 70ft. wide, and consisted of two bays covering four rows of engine pits. It served as a broad gauge running shed in the early days. In its latter days it was used for 'finishing off' work such as repairs to sand boxes, engine buffers, cleaning and painting, etc. The two commemorative carved stone tablets, representing broad gauge engines, which adorned the building, had, by the time of this photograph, been removed to the front wall of the general offices. The reason for this photograph, taken on 28th October 1929, was that the building was to be demolished under a Government loan scheme for the relief of unemployment, to make way for modernisation of the engine repair shops at Swindon.

Plate 34 (below): The size of Swindon Works in its heyday may be comprehended in this general panoramic view of the famous 'A' Erecting and Machine Shop, photographed in 1923. The shop covered an area of more than half a million square feet, and the main running lines are in the foreground of this photograph. The engine standing on the right is No. 3317 *Somerset* of the 'County' class.

Plate 35: This second panoramic view, photographed on 30th April 1908, shows the Carriage and Wagon Works management office block with No. 15 Shop backing on to it. This area was to the north-east of the main line station.

The Trimming Shop in the Carriage Works of Swindon made, as the name implies, a variety of items for use in the building of railway coaches. Many and various were the objects produced including seats, seat backs, carriage window blinds, carpets made-up, cushions, towels, window straps, overalls, aprons, signalling flags, string nets for luggage racks, leather wear such as vestibule gangways, despatch bags, tablet pouches, belts for machines, beds and covers for ambulance stretchers, hose bags for water cranes, shields for axleboxes, leather washers of all descriptions — the list is endless. What a remarkable Works — Swindon was virtually self-contained.

Plate 36: This shows the Strap Shop with many of the items listed above to be seen in the photograph. A special service of this shop was to make artificial limbs for servants of the Company who had the misfortune of losing limbs whilst working for the GWR. This service had been provided since 1878 and up to 1916, (the date of the photograph) over 4,000 items had been made.

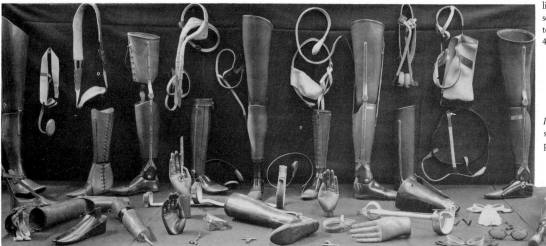

Plate 37: This view shows a comprehensive selection of what was capable of being produced.

Plate 38: Photographed is the 'new' saw mills (built June 1908), with the Ransome horizontal log band saw on the right of the picture. The overhead 10 ton travelling crane extended outside the shop, to enable quick handling of the heavy logs prior to entering the mill. The Ransome saw would cut a Baltic oak at the rate of 50ft. per minute. Other equipment in this shop consisted of a large planer, whose shavings were conveyed by a cyclone elevator into the fuel loft for use as a heating fuel.

Stations

Plate 39: The Great Western took very many photographs of their stations and this view shows Acton in 1903 on the main line out of Paddington. This fine period piece illustrates the main station buildings over the running tracks, with the signal box tucked just behind the bridge. A variety of lighting standards and enamel signs may be observed.

Plate 40: Stourbridge Junction Station ('change for Stourbridge Town') seen in 1905. The station had been rebuilt in 1901, being moved ½ mile to the south in the process. Two 700ft. island platforms were provided and the scheme cost over £60,000. An interesting set of signals stand on the right of the picture.

Plate 41: The reason for taking this photograph of Torquay is not clear. Minor work took place in 1897 when the paving on the 'up' platform (furthest from the camera) was extended, whilst in 1908 a temporary connection was inserted in the 'up' line (slightly to the left of where the workmen are standing) to enable a start to be made on the doubling of the line between Torquay and Paignton. This view, therefore, may have been taken in connection with one of those events; the period is certainly around the turn of the century.

Plate 42: This picture is full of interest, and shows the track leading into Cirencester Station, photographed around 1900. The track-work, point levers, water tank, signal box, and lattice post signals, all are worthy of detailed study.

Plate 43: Situated beneath the ornate roof of Windsor Station were the Royal waiting-rooms. The clock was of Indian style, and both rooms were lavishly wood-panelled, luxuriously carpeted and beautifully decorated. The rooms were last used for the funeral of the late King George V in 1936.

Plate 44 (right upper): Exeter St. Thomas Station had an all-over roof which provided shelter for the many thousands of passengers handled at this station every year. A railmotor service had been established by 1906 with Newton Abbot, serving the intermediate towns and seaside resorts. This fine view shows the roof construction in some detail, together with the many advertising signs. Note that the station nameboard reads 'St. Thomas'; it became 'Exeter (St. Thomas)' in May 1897, but the nameboard does not seem to have been changed in this 1904 photograph.

Plate 45 (right lower): Opposite the Duke of Cornwall Hotel stood the Great Western Railway's Plymouth (Millbay) Station, and this photograph shows the ornate forecourt station canopy with a horse and milk cart waiting, and a steam road-roller moving up the street behind. This photograph reflects the long exposure which the photographers had to use, causing the blurred movements of people within the scene.

Plate 46: A part of the official photographer's work was to produce, for the Civil Engineers, a series of working station photographs for major station reconstruction. One such set produced for Oxford has been assembled here to give some idea of the various parts of a station and its attractions. From left to right are the ladies' waiting-room, weighing machine, penny engraving machine, Nestles chocolate machine, cigarette machine, entrance barrier, ticket collector's office, Nestles machine, goods entrance, kiosk, telegraph office, stationmaster's and general enquiries office, goods entrance, post box, waiting-room, bookstall, gentlemen's lavatory, weighing machine, Nestles machine, sweet machine, mintips and penny machines, ladies' room and cloakroom, and finally the inspector's office, before the bicycle rack. A similar array of photographs was produced for Reading, Didcot, Taunton and Banbury.

Plate 47: The 'home town' of the Great Western Railway must surely be Swindon, and this view shows the old Swindon Junction Station circa 1910.

Plate 48: Southall Station at the east end showing the goods shed, engine shed and coaling station. The 2-4-0T 'Metro Tank', No. 1420, is on the local service to Paddington — a view full of GWR detail! The footbridge was erected to enable the engine shed staff to get to work without crossing the tracks.

Plate 49: The principal station at Exeter was Exeter (St. David's) which was reconstructed between 1911 and 1914. The photograph chosen to portray this shows the luggage bridge nearing completion in May 1913 to allow for 'safe and rapid' transit of luggage between the three platforms. Electrically operated lifts of 30 cwt. capacity were installed with new lattice safety gates. The contractors notes state: 'the towers were constructed with rock-faced quoins, string mouldings and cornices of Nailsworth stones with panel walls in hammer-dressed, coarse rubble work of Westleigh limestone'. The GWR arranged for a series of photographs during the 1911-14 period, to record all the stages of the station's reconstruction.

Plate 50: In connection with the GWR's remodelling of Birmingham (Snow Hill) Station, a novel device was installed to deal with incoming engines in bay platforms 3 and 4. It was called a sector table, and allowed engines to be transferred from one line to the other. This view shows the three road table and the 'pocket' under the platform into which the plate moved. The sector plate was interlocked with the signal box and was operated by an electric motor, gears and ropes. This particular table had just been installed by Ransomes & Rapier of Ipswich when this official photograph was taken in July 1911.

Plate 51: Workmen's trains were a subject of investigation by the Company in 1907, and this picture was taken by the official photographer for this reason. These trains had been introduced in 1893 and a very interesting article on this subject is published in the 1907 edition of the *GWR Magazine*. This view, photographed at Southall (Brentford Junction), illustrates the clothing worn by male and female workpeople at this time.

Plate 52: Crosskeys, on the Risca to Aberbeeg line in South Wales, photographed circa 1910, showing the two levels of platform and the unevenness of the track and site in general. The footbridge design is of interest, and the reason for the photograph could be that it is a new one.

Plate 53: Pontypool Road during its rebuilding on a new site, north of the old station, in 1909. There is a sign to the left of the extreme left-hand track which reads 'SPEED TO BE REDUCED TO 10 MILES PER HOUR'.

Plate 54: St. Agnes Station, on the Truro to Newquay branch, under construction and revealing interesting building details. This scene was photographed on 5th June 1902 and shows the contractor's track construction — somewhat crude.

Plate 55: The Government-sponsored 'Relief of Unemployment' scheme in 1929 authorised expenditure on railways, and one item of work involved quadrupling the track through Wellington Station. On 22nd April 1931 the new 'up' platform was well under way.

G.W.R.–The Holiday Line

Plate 56: This is Knowle & Dorridge Station, pictured on 31st May 1934, rebuilt as part of the quadrupling between Olton and Lapworth in 1933. The signal box pictured had also been renewed as part of the scheme.

Plate 57: This fine earlier view should be compared with that in *Plate 54* and is a 1900s' scene from the bridge overlooking Fairford Station, the terminus of the Fairford branch. These 12in. x 10in. plate glass negatives could easily be broken and, as here, repaired with tape. Many were destroyed, once broken, with the loss of many historic scenes, but happily this one survived. Although recorded in the official registers as Lechlade Station, it is obviously Fairford, showing how even GWR records can be misleading. The distant view of the water tower and engine shed, and the location of the weighbridge on the right, all tally with the official track plan of Fairford.

Plate 58: Pershore Station, between Worcester and Evesham, recorded on a 12in. x 10in. plate glass negative in 1900. This was one of several pictures taken on this line around the same date but I have not been able to ascertain if they were used for publicity or for civil engineer's purposes. Possibly the 'down' starting signal, poorly positioned beyond the bridge, is to be re-sited at the platform end (note the white background painted on the bridge), and the photograph was taken to record its previous location. The 'up' home signal is very tall, so that it can be seen above the bridge from a reasonable distance. The station appears to be very well cared for.

Plate 59: This view illustrates the new station at Olton that was provided for the quadrupling of the track. Note the style of lettering on the station front, similar to other stations such as Abingdon.

Holiday Haunts

In 1906 the first *Holiday Haunts* Guide was issued, and each year thereafter, up to 1916, a new edition was produced by which time the circulation had grown to 50,000 copies. It was revived after the war (in 1921) and appeared regularly in March every year until 1947. In 1933, the pages had grown to 1,032, including 629 pages of adverts and 184 pages of illustrations, and over 200,000 copies were sold annually at 6d apiece! To produce an 'annual' of this size involved many people and again our official photographers were pressed into action, taking many thousands of non-railway subjects. Each city on the GWR was covered, and places like Bath, Bristol, Oxford, Stratford-upon-Avon, Taunton and Plymouth had their landmarks recorded, many of the photographs dating back to the 1920s. In the next few plates some of these classics have been reproduced, but many more are in the GWR collection awaiting to be seen.

Plate 60: This is a typical view, photographed in the early 1920s by the staff photographer. This scene at Clifton Hampden, on the Thames, shows the Barley Mow public house, still in use today as a restaurant. The scene has changed little, although the costumes have — all in all a nostalgic photograph of high quality.

Plate 61: The Isis or River Thames at Oxford, photographed in June 1936 to capture the College barges. These, alas, have now all disappeared and so this photograph only revives distant memories and the splendour of the scene.

Plate 62: The village harbour scene at St. Ives seems to indicate a fishing boat berthing problem, and reminds us just how active the industry was in the 1930s. A sight never to be repeated.

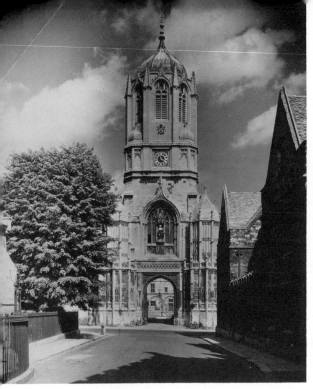

Plate 63: Architectural photography was carried out by the staff photographers and Oxford was represented by many pictures of the colleges. This photograph shows Christ Church College (Tom Tower) in all its glory in June 1936. It is of interest to note that in 1842 Sir Daniel Gooch repaired the weathercock to this tower in the GWR workshop at Swindon. This repair included adding new bearings to the spindle to allow better rotation of the 1 cwt vane.

Plate 64: The Thames was obviously a favourite haunt and here at Marsh Lock can be seen a conglomeration of punts, with boaters and parasols in profusion on what appears to be a fine summer's afternoon.

Plate 65: 'Fisherwomen, somewhere in Wales', is all the negative registers say for this print, dated 1890. One wonders why an official GWR photograph was taken, and can only presume it was at a dock or harbour belonging to the Company.

Plate 66: The last look at the *Holiday Haunts* series of photographs shows Newquay harbour in July 1923 with its harbour railway system. Wagons were let down by a ropeway through a tunnel from the yard above, to the harbour. A weighbridge is situated in the white building on the right. How the wagons were moved around the harbour complex is not obvious, but as they were pulled by horses from the station to the top of the incline, it is pretty certain that horses were used at the harbour as well.

Publicity

Publicity within the Great Western was probably some of the finest company publicity ever seen in Britain. Their own monthly staff magazine (not equalled in my estimation in context and presentation by any other railway company) ran from 1888 to 1947 (nationalisation). Even during the war years it continued to be produced, even if the index in one year was handwritten. The Company produced many fine and famous publications throughout its life, recording not only its engineering achievements but cultural and social happenings within its territory.

Plates 67, 68 & 69: Posters were a major part of the publicity output, and the GWR commissioned many famous artists and designers to maintain the high standard which the GWR required. Literally thousands of posters, handbills, and pamphlets, etc. were produced and here is just a mouthwatering sample of the quality and subjects chosen (*see also introduction page*).

Plate 70: The publicity department also produced portable show stands for exhibitions, not only in Great Britain but overseas, and the items needed were made and prepared at Swindon Works. Pictured here is the material ready for a Manchester Exhibition in July 1913. The three boards depict (a) The Holiday Line; (b) The Progressive Line; (c) a full relief map of the GWR.

Plates 71 & 72 (right): The staff photographer obviously became very involved in the production of the many publicity stunts, and these pictures show two 'posed' passenger photographs of widely-separated periods. These two views do allow the fine details of coach livery and lettering to be examined.

Plate 73 (below): This is a typical publicity photograph, and shows how the designer has 'masked' the negative to the area he required for the particular brochure. Much can be gleaned from these posed pictures, particularly on the dress of the day.

Plate 74: Another trade stand mock-up, photographed at Swindon Works in 1902 for an exhibition in the Midlands. Do look at the superb craftsmanship in the scroll headboard, and the two beautiful models; one of a new twin screw steel steamship representing the 'Great Western' and 'Great Southern' (express service between New Milford and Waterford, Ireland), and the other a cut-away model of a tender locomotive. Even this photograph has been retouched by blanking out all the background, and was obviously used in publicity material. The stand was still in use in 1911 when it was seen at the Scottish National Exhibition which was visited by over a million people.

Plate 75: 'Publicity' also meant offices around the system where timetables, tickets, and reservations, etc. could be purchased by the traveller, and here the Great Western never missed a trick. Here we see the sparse Great Western Railway Office at White Rock, on Guernsey in the Channel Islands, photographed in June 1925.

Plate 76 (right): This photograph was taken again at Swindon Works, but this time in 1914 and shows the Company's 'Enquiry Kiosk'. Used at the Bath & West Show, the Welsh National Eisteddfod, and many similar venues, it was said to have been the 'most handsome building on the ground'. It certainly is a superb example of woodworking and painting skill from the craftsmen of Swindon.

Company Publications

Plates 77 to 81: A selection of page headings from the Great Western staff magazine *(right)*. This shows the changes in typography through the years. Books 'For boys of all ages' were issued by the GWR Publicity Department in the 1920s and 1930s, and the evocative cover designs are shown above. These books were enormously popular, with huge numbers being sold and many editions published. Copies of part of a sales brochure *The Literature of Locomotion* are also shown. This was issued by the GWR Publicity Department to advertise its products. Books, jigsaws and posters all feature. Finally, is a reproduction of the cover of one of the most famous books issued by the company *The Cornish Riviera* by S. P. B. Mais.

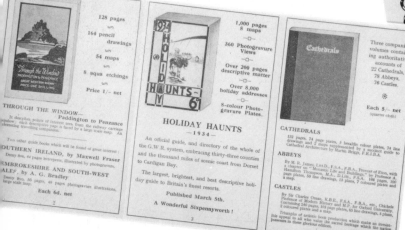

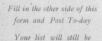

World War I Work at Swindon Works

From the previously mentioned laundry work and the making of artificial limbs, etc., the manufacture of war munitions was a far cry, but it serves to illustrate the remarkable adaptability of the Great Western Railway Engineering Workshops at Swindon. During World War I, the GWR at Swindon manufactured ambulance trains, gun carriages, ammunition wagons and other vehicles, shell fuses, cartridge cases, and spare parts for locomotives used in France. This was all produced without any financial profit whatever to the Company. During this period over 63,000 special freight trains and over 3,000 special troop trains were run (including 6,000 loaded ambulance trains). *Plates 82 to 89* show some of the official photographs taken at this time to record the events.

Plate 82 (top): Locomotive No. 2250 in charge of the train of the four 6in. guns seen in *Plates 88 & 89*.

Plate 83 (right): Another magnificent gun within Swindon Works. The wagon is interesting as it has 'R.A.F. 87' in old paint on the side, and appears not of GWR design.

Plate 84 (right): A further type of field gun (8in. Howitzer) with shell loading hoist, ready for despatch. The stone broad gauge engine plaque (previously mentioned) can be seen in the top right of the picture.

Plate 85 (below): These guns await loading on to the wagons. There is an interesting collection of engines, crane and wagons standing nearby.

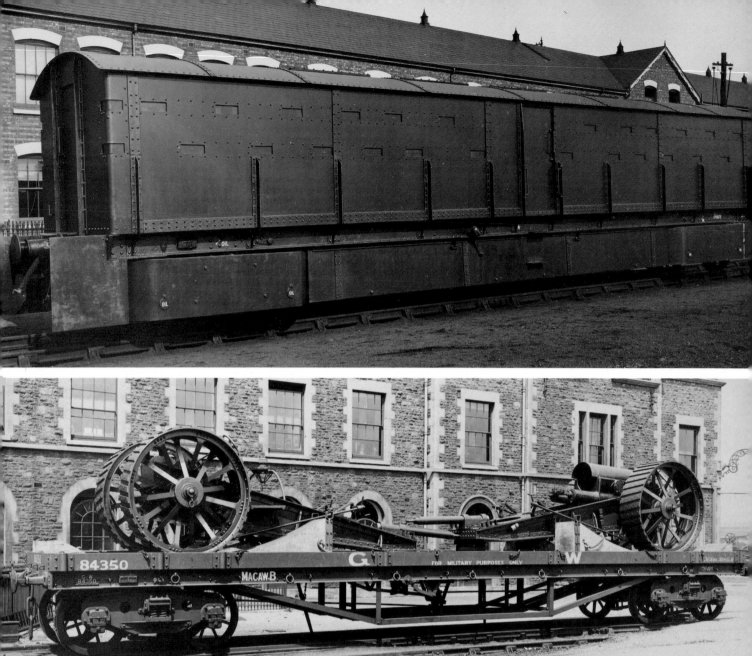
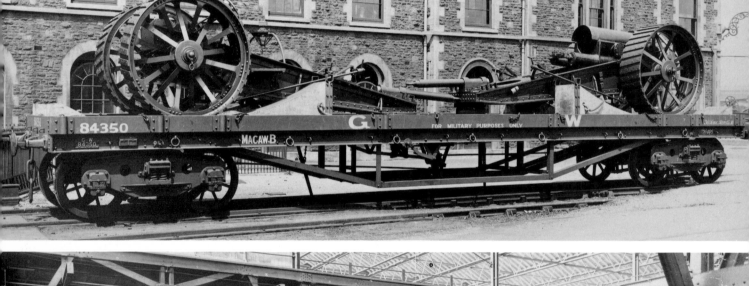

84350   MACAW.B   G   FOR MILITARY PURPOSES ONLY   W

Plate 89: A final publicity photograph of the finished product with the guns ready pointing skyward, strapped on to the *'Macaw B'* bogie wagons outside the main offices at Swindon Works. It need hardly be reported that when war was declared, 25,000 GWR men heeded the call to arms (nearly 32 per cent of the pre-war staff) and the number killed amounted to 2,524, with 600 war medals being awarded for bravery.

The GWR in World War II

World War II brought many people — strange to each other, and strangely assorted — together as neighbours, in adjacent shelters, bunkers or makeshift homes such as the London Tube platforms. Swindon Works also shared the strange experience of wagons laid alongside landing craft, midget submarines, guns, shells, bombs, armour plate, cranes, searchlights, with military repairs being carried out alongside locomotives, and gun carriages replacing railway carriage production. The next series of photographs captures some of the wartime atmosphere and activity within the GWR.

Plates 90 & 91: These views show how the GWR provided air raid shelters around the system — sparse but effective.

Plate 86 (left upper): An armoured railway wagon at Swindon Works (showing the door and rifle holes shut). These vehicles were supplied to the East Coast area during the war. The noise inside with a possible 50 rifles able to be discharged must have been ear-shattering. Note the provision for oiling, and the bulletproof protection for the couplings and buffers.

Plate 87 (left middle): Two 8in. Howitzer gun carriages loaded ready for despatch outside the main Swindon Works offices. Note the magnificent wall lamp.

Plate 88 (left lower): Gun manufacture alongside locomotive work in the Boiler Shop, in the heart of Swindon Works; 6in. guns and travelling carriages are being assembled. Note the tare weight painted on gun No. 12 is 2 tons, 13 cwts 3 quarters.

Plate 92 (above): The main stations could obviously not be protected but blast proof sand-bagging around windows and offices did afford some protection as seen at Birmingham (Snow Hill).

Plates 93, 94 & 95: To cater for the increase in fire risk due to the hazards of incendiary bombs in time of war, the Company supplied petrol-driven trailer pumps *(Plate 93)*. Increased training of personnel to man these systems was called for and more frequent fire fighting practice sessions *(Plate 94)*. The dustbin inside the vehicle *(Plate 93)* contained sand for use on incendiary bombs. With war, the need for ambulances and first aiders increased, and so the Company converted many vehicles into ambulances *(Plate 95)* training the crews in gas warfare drill. Notice the Morris Commercial lorry still advertises 'Glorious Devon' for your holidays! These photographs were all taken for the staff magazine to boost the morale of all the staff during these difficult years. The particular vehicle shown was a 2 ton Morris Commercial vehicle fitted with a Swindon body, No. 2399. The headlights had black-out masks and the edges of the wings were painted white, as required by wartime regulations.

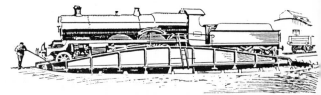

Plate 96: It was not widely known that the Luftwaffe managed to bomb Swindon Works, but on 26th July 1942, bombs did fall near the Works as can be seen in this scene. One direct hit and one unexploded bomb are marked in this official photograph by the photographic department for the report to the Directors.

Plate 97: Swindon was chosen to produce the first 2,000 and 4,000lb. bombs as the railway workshops were suitable to manufacture the cases. One Friday in October 1940, a GWR representative was summoned to London, and by the following Wednesday the bombs had been manufactured. The first twelve bombs were used in essential tests, and one bomb was used purely as a dimension test model in the aircraft. Several were filled with sand and sawdust to the correct weight for flight testing and ground-hitting pattern; others were exploded electrically on the ground for explosive effects and, lastly, several were dropped for final 'live' tests. When tested, another 80 were supplied immediately for live filling. Some of these were used in the Essen raids and such was their success that 2,032 more big bombs were produced during World War II.

Plate 98: This shows the loading of 250lb. bombs (eight at a time) in 'X' Shop on 20th December 1940. Swindon managed to produce 83,000 of these before this type was phased out in favour of the 500lb. general purpose bomb. Each production line for these bombs consisted of five lathes, two other specialist machines, a varnishing oven, and an assembly bench.

Plates 99, 100 & 101: Secret at the time, but hundreds of Swindon men knew about the sensational construction of two men midget submarines. This work during 1942/3 was carried out in the No. 7 Woodworking Shop of the Carriage Works and was undertaken to assist a West of England firm that had suffered from an air attack. The superstructure was made of wood *(Plate 99)* and had to be to a high standard to withstand the 90p.s.i. of water pressure when submerged. *Plate 100* shows the steering fins and propulsion fan, and *Plate 101* the finished superstructure with curtains fitted to protect the submariners who rode astride these strange craft on their perilous missions. Over fifty of these craft were completed by Swindon.

Plate 102 (below): Another look at the 4,000lb. bomb, fitted with rollers and being moved into 'L2' Shop in October 1941. The authorities were worried that the lugs on these 2 ton bombs might give way as they were flown over English cities. Swindon rose to the occasion and tested the lugs to a strain of 16 tons, (eight times the bomb's weight), and on to 22 tons before the testing gear gave way, and not the lug!

Plate 103 (below): The mountings for the 6 pounder Hotchkiss guns were also developed and built at Swindon, and in 1941 a Naval captain illustrated the type of stand required by cutting paper and wrapping it round his thumb, folding it up and bending out the legs. The trick looked simple, but to repeat it in steel plate an inch thick was not so easy. The response was again swift, and the first two guns were finished and despatched within a week. This scene was photographed in 'W' Shop on 5th August 1941.

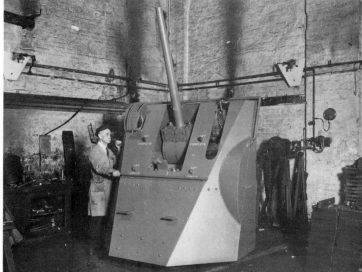

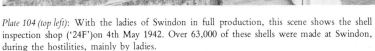

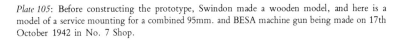

Plate 104 (top left): With the ladies of Swindon in full production, this scene shows the shell inspection shop ('24F')on 4th May 1942. Over 63,000 of these shells were made at Swindon, during the hostilities, mainly by ladies.

Plate 105: Before constructing the prototype, Swindon made a wooden model, and here is a model of a service mounting for a combined 95mm. and BESA machine gun being made on 17th October 1942 in No. 7 Shop.

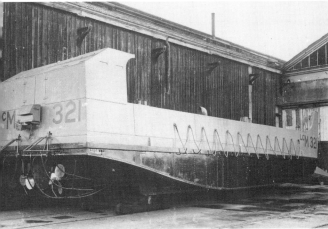

Plate 106 (left): The 'Inland Shipyard' was the nickname for '13' Shop (Wagon Frame Shop) where the motor landing craft (MLC) were constructed. It was also another 'first' for the GWR as it was the first time this type of vessel had been constructed on jigs. These large craft, 40ft. long by 13ft. 6in. wide, were about as big as could be fully assembled inland, and were later known as LCM (landing craft, mechanical). The first order for twelve came in August 1941, and No. 1 was delivered in May 1942. From then onwards, one left Swindon by road every eight days. This photograph was taken in February 1943, and shows the new code letters LCM (the reason for this photograph).

With a healthy stock of boilers, the GWR pressed 'V' Shop into preparing bulletproof steel. This comprised of machining, levelling and tempering bulletproof sheets for armoured vehicles. Each vehicle needed 261 plates of 169 different shapes and sizes, and with ninety vehicles completed, 'V' Shop produced 23,490 overall plates. The final test for each batch of plates was a bullet test, so the GWR constructed its own rifle range near the boiler shop.

Plate 107: This shows the results of one of these tests in May 1941; quite conclusive. One report said that a special jeep (crew and all) rushed into Swindon, still covered in dust from the front, and had to be armour-plated for a special mission. Within a few hours the job was complete and the jeep and crew were away on board a transport plane to the Continent.

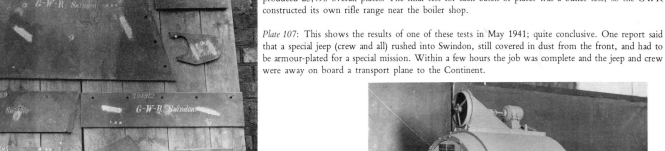

109 (above): The gallant ladies of Swindon are seen welding superheater units in 'P1' Shop 1th March 1942. Without the help of the female work-force, many shops would have been pressed to cope in those nerve-racking years.

Plate 108 (above): Many other items of war were produced; here is a projector searchlight with special caterpillar track wheels, assembled at Swindon in 1941.

Thirty four dock cranes, six 3 ton hydraulic cranes, many repairs for aircraft firms, and loaning a resurfacing machine to an aerodrome for runway repairs were among the infinite variety of jobs that Swindon were to carry out. But the attitude, determination and skills of the men and women of the Great Western Works at Swindon was summed up by the quote 'if it's difficult, we'll do it immediately; if it's impossible, it may take a little longer'. Well done, Swindon!

Plate 111 (above): This is of interest as it is all that remained of a coach of the 4.52p.m Salisbury to Bristol train. Photographed at the Bath end of No. 2 tunnel, Foxes Wood, on 6th December 1940, it shows how the bomb struck the face of the tunnel and ricocheted into the coach. The result was quite amazing!

Plate 110: The protection of Swindon Works from air attack was obviously essential and many anti-aircraft gun positions were established around the complex. In this view the Swindon Junction Station post can be seen on 3rd March 1941. A good loco-spotting position as well!

Obviously the Great Western suffered a great deal of war damage and included are *Plates, 111, 112 & 113* to show some of the problems the staff had to cope with.

Plates 112 (below) & 113 (opposite top left): This shows the extensive damage due to bombing at Castle Cary on 3rd September 1942. The engine, No. 1729, an 0-6-0T, suffered badly and the new signal box, goods shed and many wagons were totally destroyed by direct hits. The man standing by the lever frame with his hands in his pocket sums up the situation; 'what do we do first?'

Plate 114 (top right): With the hostilities gathering momentum, the GWR set about converting, constructing and fitting out ambulance trains. The first to be completed was handed over on 24th March 1943 at Swindon Works by Mr. F. W. Hawksworth (Chief Mechanical Engineer to the Great Western Railway from 1941-1949). Each train comprised six ward carriages and a sitting-up carriage for patients, giving a total capacity for about 300. There were also two carriages for medical officers, nurses and attendants, and two catering carriages. A further vehicle was equipped with an operating theatre and pharmacy, and finally a brake carriage incorporated boiler heating facilities, and another brake end vehicle and stores section brought the total to fourteen vehicles — a complete hospital on wheels.

Plate 115 (above): The outside of the vehicles were painted khaki, with grey roofs, and in the centre on the top was painted a large red cross on a white background, with a smaller version on each side. The coaches were equipped with chemical toilets, hot water and heating, and special jacking sockets for lifting on to ferry boats *(see Plate 159)*. This scene shows the handing-over ceremony to Brig. Gen. Hawley of the US Army with 'Movietone' present.

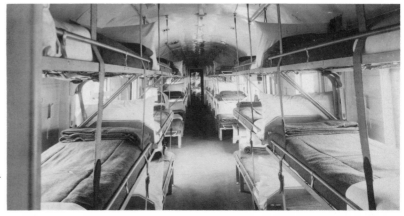

Plate 116: The interior of one of the ward cars.

Road Vehicles

Plate 117: Photographed outside The Royal Inn at Beaconsfield in Buckinghamshire in 1904 is one of the early GWR motor omnibus services. The first GWR service between Helston and The Lizard used a Milnes-Daimler 16hp petrol-engined 22 seat motor omnibus. This was replaced on 12th November 1903 by No. 1 (a similar bus to No. 5, seen here) which could carry eighteen passengers and up to 15 cwt. of luggage. The interior was lit by one acetylene lamp, and at night the car carried five headlights. The new service, photographed in April 1904, was between Slough and Beaconsfield and gave 'unbounded' satisfaction in the districts served, and the cars were always well-filled. The livery is interesting as it is certainly non standard.

Plate 118: This is a posed view at the South Lambeth depot of horse transport. Horses were widely used within the GWR system, and keen competition existed between depots to obtain the 'Horse of the Year' award. Looking at the wagon loads in the background, these animals earned their keep.

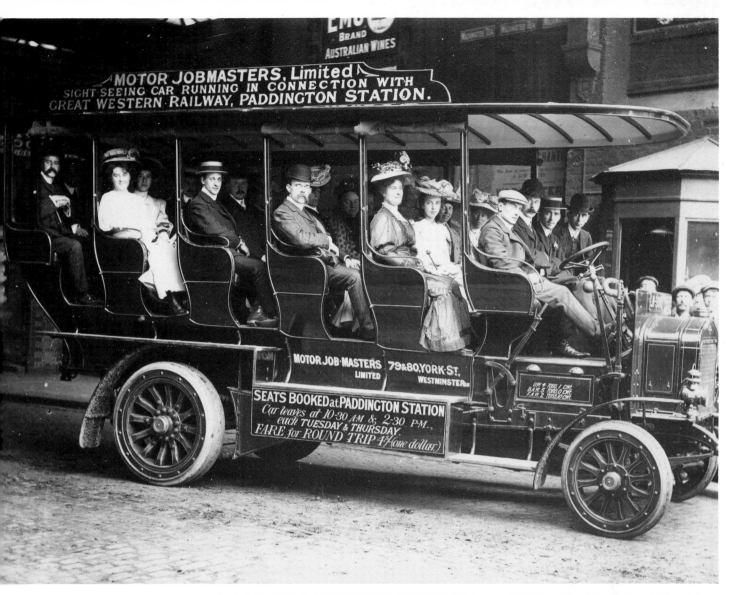

Plate 119: This fine period photograph, taken by the official photographer of the GWR, is really self-explanatory. 'Motor Job-Masters Ltd. 79 & 80, York Street Westminster. Sight seeing car running in connection with the Great Western Railway, Paddington Station'. The fare: 4/-. or one dollar (that's five dollars to the pound!).

Plate 120: The Great Western did not waste an opportunity and when the motor vehicle became widely available, started to use surplus cars for advertising purposes. Here we see both *Holiday Haunts* and 'The Cornish Riviera' being widely advertised.

Plate 121: It was not surprising that the GWR owned a church, or rather a building that once was a church. They purchased, in 1901, All Saints Church in Tyndall Street, Cardiff, and used it as a powerhouse, oil store and warehouse before converting it to a motor vehicle repair shop in 1929; an inspection pit replacing the pulpit! The building housed twelve lorries and workshop equipment. In this photograph, taken on the 14th May 1936, note the 'ghost' tyre due to the long exposure required, someone having removed the tyre during the proceedings.

Plate 122: This photograph was taken on 17th March 1925 and illustrates an AEC 3½ ton saloon omnibus No. 228 (Regn. No. T8148) waiting in the station yard at Kingsbridge; the vehicle was rebuilt as a lorry in 1926. The older type of omnibus was often used on the 'sleepy' branch terminus services.

Plate 123: The 1906 electric delivery vehicle introduced by the GWR in that year (loaded with cigarettes). This vehicle was capable of carrying 2 tons and was propelled by two electric motors from an 80 volt battery source. No. 95, seen here, was built at the Slough Workshops of the GWR and had a range of about 30 miles on one charge. The braking was on the electric motor shaft, and the ingenious calipers can clearly be seen in front of the rear soled rubber wheels.

Plate 124: With so many horses employed on railway duties at Paddington goods depot, the Company converted an old building, used for minting coins, into a two storey stables, called the Mint Stables, and access to the top floor was by a ramp from the cobbled courtyard. Again the official photographer seems to have caught a very orderly and well-spaced row of horses and men for his picture.

Plate 125: Another publicity posed photograph to be used for a special advert which appeared in the *Railway Gazette* and *GWR Magazine* in 1935. This photograph, taken at Cardiff, was captioned: 'Although it is early morning, the Railhead Fleet is ready for the road' — and what a mixed fleet it was!

Plate 126: One of the garages looking after the road fleet in the London area was the Alfred Road garage at Westbourne Park. This 1934 view shows a variety of vehicles and interesting signs. From left to right: a 4 ton Thornycroft, an FD chassis high-bodied lorry; No. 2741, a 3 ton mechanical horse built by Scammell; a 4/5 ton Daimler No. 1922 is seen going into the garage, and horse wagon No. 2251 is on the extreme right. One notice on the wall states 'No drivers in this shop' whilst the sign on the petrol pump boom reads 'Remember, no racing on a cold engine — *DON'T FORGET YOUR PETROL BONUS'.* Drivers at this time were paid to save petrol, in a bonus scheme — perhaps this scheme should be revived!

Plate 127: Container traffic increased immensely in the late 1930s and 1940s, and here, photographed at Action Yard, on 9th September 1947, is a 6 ton Scammell 3-wheel tractor, No. C6318, with a 6 ton trailer, No. T6499. The name *'DYAK-G'* on the trailer was a railway telegraphic code name, similar to that used on wagons. The refrigerated container, obviously used by Wall's ice cream was coded 'AF' and numbered 2103.

Station Trolleys

Plate 128 (left): From road vehicles to hand-drawn vehicles, this first photograph shows a fire cart fitted with 'Radium' fire extinguishers, and is pictured at Paddington Station in 1911. This vehicle was necessary due to the large amount of motor traffic passing in and out of Paddington Station, and the new risk of a petrol fire.

Plate 129 (below): 'At your service, Madam!'; with sugar from a silver bowl, this platform trolley was rather 'up market'. The 1939 *GWR Magazine* stated that these platform buffets were in great demand as the restaurant cars at this time had been withdrawn from the trains. The crockery on the trolley has the GWR monogram roundel. The trolley contains a selection of Players and Craven 'A' cigarettes, with chocolates by Cadbury's, crisps by Smith's, beef and ham sandwiches, plus fruit and drinks; the selection was better than the modern equivalent and much cheaper in comparison.

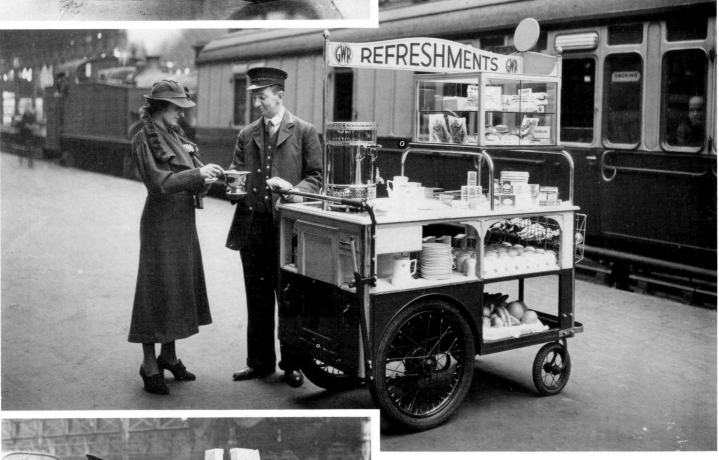

Plate 130 (left): Station platform service, on the large main line stations, was an important public relations act by the GWR, and was controlled by the buffet and restaurant manager. The well-equipped trolley seen is at Paddington Station in 1922, and has amongst its wares GWR snack boxes, fruit, cakes, sandwiches, cigarettes, chocolates and, of course, tea, coffee and minerals. The highly-polished urn was split into two sections, one for coffee and one for tea, and these trolleys were usually manned by the younger buffet staff in training!

Plate 131 *(left)*: Another trolley, this time seen at Paddington on 18th January 1927, but only selling fruit. Bananas 1½d. each, dessert apples 1½d. each, oranges 1½d. each, boxed dates, pineapples, grapes, tangerines and pears —what a choice!

Station Kiosks

Plate 132: Other station facilities were also an important feature of GWR stations, and kiosks were often highly sought after by local tradesmen. Portrayed here is Wyman the Newsagent at Paddington Station. The abundance of notices is interesting (possibly overdone), and one suspects that the GWR poster on the right has been pinned up especially for the official photographer. The *GWR Magazine* hangs up for sale as do the GWR timetables. A new GWR publication *Handy Aids to Travel* (2d) is hanging down in strips and the posters on display around the bookstall tell us a great deal about the literature of 1913.

Plate 133: Empire Fruit Stores Ltd. kiosk at Paddington, photographed on 15th July 1927, is featured in this view. With three staff to serve, the stall notice states: 'Our speciality. When in season and in good condition EAT EMPIRE FRUIT. We ask the consuming public to give voluntary preference to fruit grown within the Empire and to ask for same from the assistant'. The Nestle's vending machine on the left is worthy of a glance.

Refreshment Rooms

Plate 134: The main refreshment rooms at stations were also greatly prized by the Company and Birmingham (Snow Hill) Station's main refreshment room is pictured on 13th August 1926. Fresh flowers, mosaic floor, stained glass windows and Company crested crockery, all help to create an air of cleanliness and efficiency.

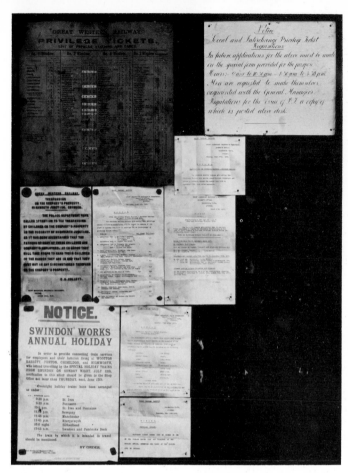

For many people the 'trip' also meant a honeymoon. The organisation was immense, with trains marshalled around the Works, carriage sidings and the station. Each needed to be labelled and special buses and taxis had to be arranged to move the passengers in from outlying villages and suburbs of Swindon to catch the overnight services to Penzance, Newquay, etc. Even perambulators, bicycles and dogs were catered for! With all this excitement, Swindon traders also rose to the occasion advertising 'Bargains for trip'.

Plate 135: One wonders why the notice board at Swindon Works was the subject of an official photograph, unless this was a new site for the said board. However, the photograph reveals a great deal about privilege tickets and also the Works Annual Holiday (dealt with in *Plates 136, 137, 138 & 139*). The notices tell of fares available on the privilege ticket; e.g. Brighton 7s. 0d., Hastings 8s. 9d., or locally, Steventon 1s. 4d., Stratton 3d., Newbury 3s. 3d., or Melksham 1s. 5½d., etc. A Police notice also warns parents that children of Company employees are playing on the line at Highworth Junction. Another notice cancels the use of the privilege tickets on the Underground on 28th June 1930 because of a large aerial pageant at Colindale. A further notice warns employees that unless their ticket warrants are signed before being presented, the issue of a ticket will be refused! The last but most important poster is the one on the lower left — 'Swindon Works Annual Holiday' and reads:

In order to provide connecting train services for employees and their families living at WOOTTON BASSETT, PURTON, CHISELDON, and HIGHWORTH, who intend travelling by the SPECIAL HOLIDAY TRAINS FROM SWINDON ON SUNDAY NIGHT, JULY 13th, notification to this effect should be given to the Shop Office not later than THURSDAY, next, June 12th.

Overnight holiday trains have been arranged as under:

SWINDON DEPT	TO
9.30p.m.	St. Ives
9.50p.m.	Penzance
10.05p.m.	St. Ives and Penzance
11.10p.m.	Newquay
11.45p.m.	Manchester
11.45p.m.	Aberystwyth
12.00 night	Birkenhead
12.15a.m.	Swansea and Pembroke Dock

The train by which it is intended to travel should be mentioned.

Chief Mechanical Engineer's Office
Swindon June 7th, 1930

BY ORDER

The *GWR Magazine* reported:

Once a year it came (since the first Special in 1849) and the trouble always started in exactly the same way as it did each year — that is to say, just when Bill Smith (or as the registers would have it, William Henry Smith, 0042, 4X Shop, Swindon Loco. Works), took the form preferred to him, looked at it, and grunted: 'Trip again, eh? referring in that apparently unintelligible remark to the approach of the Swindon Works Annual Holiday'.

After filling it in, as did about 12,000 other men for any of the places offered, he would return it, six weeks in advance of the 'trip'. The GWR was then confronted with organising the travelling accommodation of around 27,000 people (about half the population of Swindon) to every part of the system, using approximately 30 special trains.

In 1934 the places most favoured by the staff are given below:

Weymouth	4,559
Paddington	4,041
Weston-super-Mare	3,606
Barry Island	1,760
St. Ives	1,196
Portsmouth	905
Teignmouth	826
North Wales	818
Paignton	783
Blackpool	728
Exmouth	622
Newquay	593
Tenby	582
Penzance	539
Jersey	463

Plate 136 (opposite): A photograph taken early in the morning of a 'trip'.

Plate 137: This shows people coming out of every road and house, all heading towards the railway and into the Works, to find their 'special'.

Plates 138 & 139: Finally the group has assembled, the coach has been found, friends made, and the final official photograph is taken before the off *(Plate 139)*. Galvanised buckets and spades are in abundance — were the buckets made at Swindon, I wonder?

Bicycles

Plate 140: It was said that bicycles were taken on the 'trip', and the GWR made a special padded blanket to go between rows of cycles to protect them on the journey, and here No. 680 Cycle Protector is seen in place. Note the acetylene bicycle lamp, front brake block and no mudguards.

GWR

TOURIST TICKET FACILITIES

MAY 1st to OCTOBER 31st, 1935

JAMES MILNE | FROM SOUTH WALES AND MONMOUTHSHIRE | General Manager

Permanent Way

A large portion of a railway's equipment obviously relates to the permanent way, and the next section looks at some of the aspects of this part of the company's system and work.

Plate 141: The junction at the west end of Reading Station is shown in this view. The main line to Bristol leaves to centre left of the picture and the West of England line enters at the bottom right.

Plate 142: This view was photographed from the new signal box on 15th May 1928, and shows the complex trackwork and crossovers at the entrance to the Queen Street Station at Cardiff during realignment.

Plate 143: The main line section outside Slough Station that formed the junction with the Windsor Branch was relayed on 29th March 1936. The old track and ballast has been cleared and the new formation assembled in the locomotive shed yard on the left. In this photograph, the new track is being manhandled on three support rails to its permanent site by the permanent way gang.

Plate 144: The Company carried out tests on the various fishplates and rail supplied. This particular test, in February 1900, shows tests on 95lb. bullhead rail joints with a drop weight of 1 ton. The various heights of the drop are clearly marked on each rail section. The state of the joint and rail is significantly different in each test.

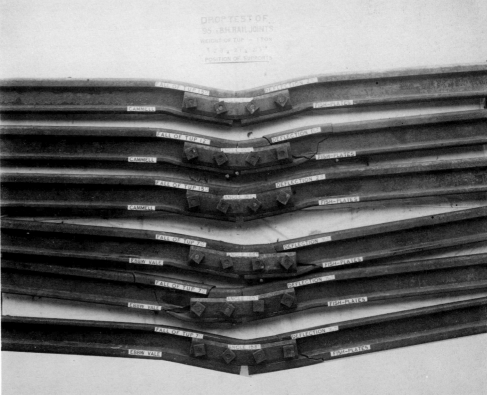

Permanent Way Maintenance

Plate 145: Photographed in November 1894, looking northwards from the Abingdon Road bridge, near Oxford, showing the awful floods of that year which lasted for weeks. A Board of Trade report makes interesting reading as to the way the GWR coped with this problem:

'On the evening in question, the trains from London were unusually late. The delay was caused at Oxford in consequence of the floods from the very great quantity of rain which had fallen, having rendered a portion of the line impassable for engines, in consequence of which it was necessary to draw the trains through the water by means of horses. The trains from London were stopped at Kennington Crossing between 2 and 3 miles south of the Oxford Station and about a quarter of a mile south of the water. The engine was here shifted to the rear of the carriages, which it pushed to the water's edge; horses were then harnessed to them, and the carriages drawn by them through the water. At the other side an engine which was to take the train on from Oxford was in waiting; this engine was accompanied by a pilotman, who received his instructions from an Inspector of Police, who was stationed on the south side of the water. The actual time required to pass a train through the water was about 12 minutes'.

Plate 146 (above left): Obviously, on branch lines, a single ganger would be in charge of quite a length of track and, to speed up his inspections, the Company devised several trolleys. This trolley was operated by a push-pull movement of the handle which was coupled to the back wheel via a crank, and it was reported, 'could move rapidly'. Note the hammer and large spanner on the cross arm. This photograph was taken on the Fairford branch near Cassington Halt.

Plate 147 (above right): If maintenance involved replacement of sleepers, then a more substantial platelayers' trolley was needed and this shows a type used. This was still light enough to be lifted off the track to allow passage of the trains.

Plate 148 (left): A screw lifting jack, which allowed the track to be lifted so that packing could be pushed into the problem area. The men featured in this photograph are certainly rugged, strong and loyal Company servants. Note the variety of headgear.

Plate 149: New track and junction being laid, and signal gantries being erected for the wartime Gloucester to Cheltenham doubling, as seen on 25th August 1942 and photographed from the signal box. Note the new telegraph posts, now a thing of the past, and also the old signal posts, one of which is laying across the new tracks.

Plate 150: Lastly, in this section, this photograph covers another 'first' for the GWR. A siding into the British Electric Transformer Company's premises at Hayes had to cross a busy road. Because a normal level crossing required large corner posts, which in this case would obstruct existing footpaths, the GWR used a Continental 'curtain' type barrier. The four barriers could be raised in twenty seconds, and were operated by a steel rod passing in an oil-filled 2½in. pipe under the road. The official photographer has, on 21st July 1930, managed to attract a reasonable crowd (many from the Railway Arms), to watch a demonstration of this novel crossing barrier.

Special Trains

Plate 151: The Great Western Royal Train of 1890 with the 2-2-2 locomotive No. 55 *Queen* at its head. The passenger vehicles are; passenger brake No. 473, first class saloon No. 316, saloon with guard's compartment, the Queen's carriage of 1874 design, an eight-wheeled first saloon, two six-wheeled passenger saloons, and a four-wheeled passenger van.

Plate 152: The new corridor train designed by Mr Dean, and constructed at Swindon Carriage Works, ran six journeys a week between Paddington and Birkenhead. After this photograph was taken in 1892 with 2-2-2 locomotive No. 3003 in charge, the 40ft. guard's van shown was replaced by a specially constructed 50ft. long vehicle to match the four other 50ft. vehicles. The first vehicle (after the guard's van) was a third class carriage, with guard's and luggage compartment; the second vehicle was third class with a smoking saloon; the third coach conveyed first class passengers with a smoking saloon; and the last one was a second class carriage with a luggage compartment and smoking saloon. The whole train had a corridor, flexible gangway connections and toilet rooms (one for ladies at one end, and one for gentlemen at the other end). A separate cubicle was set aside for ladies alongside the ladies' toilets. The lighting was by compressed oil gas in the clerestory roof, and to call the guard, an electric bell push was provided in each compartment.

Plate 153: With the introduction of the 20 ton coal wagons in 1924 to the South Wales shipment traffic, another 'first' was notched up by the GWR. The first wagons were used on 26th August 1924, when fifty wagons reached Maesteg. Seen here are fifty of the new wagons at Llandeilo Junction on a dull day, posed for the official photographer. Another photographer can be seen at the top of the signal post (just behind the tender).

Plate 154: The Royal Train again, but this time the 1897-built formation seen with 'Saint' class 4-6-0, No. 2930 *Saint Vincent*, immaculately turned out, even to the highly-polished buffers. Note the crested crown Royal headlamp standing in the centre of the front buffer beam, and the smaller than usual Royal crests on the side.

Plate 155: This is obviously a special load but just what it is I have not been able to discover, and the negative register is no help. No. 3565 is a 2-4-0T 'Metro' class locomotive, so named because they were built to work over the Metropolitan Railway, and were fitted with condensing apparatus. The locomotive was built in 1894 and was withdrawn in 1936.

Plate 156: Another sphere in which the Great Western lead the way was in the use of diesel railcars. The new AEC streamlined railcar is about to leave platform 2 at Paddington Station on a Press and Directors' run on 1st December 1933, before being put into service in early 1934. Note the railcar driver in his clean white uniform; one wonders what comments were being passed by the driver and fireman of the 'King' class locomotive alongside.

Plate 157: This is a posed photograph of a coal train on the Western Valley section in South Wales, showing more than sixty coal wagons being conveyed to the docks. These wagons had end door flaps which were secured by an iron catch at the bottom of the flap. When undone, and when the wagon was tipped, the door fell open and discharged the coal into the hoist, which stood alongside the ship.

Plate 158: 'Bulldog' class locomotive No. 3434 *Joseph Shaw* waits to leave Reading for the capital as 'Castle' class 4-6-0, No. 5018 *St. Mawes Castle* hurries through on the 'up' main line in July 1935.

Plate 159: During World War II, the GWR built two ambulance trains for the United Kingdom Flour Millers Association, who paid for their use. This train, known as 'No. 16' by the War Office, had to be shipped to France. To enable it to be lifted on to the ship, the Company experimented with lifting points, and the kitchen car is seen being lift tested by a steam crane in Swindon Works.

Plate 160: In 1947, with the awful winter causing chaos, the GWR (in conjunction with the National Gas Turbine Establishment) experimented with a gas turbine aero engine, similar to those used in the RAF Meteor fighter planes. These tests were carried out at Dowlais Top, where heavy snow drifts still persisted. The jets were bolted to a 'conflat' wagon, with their 8ft. exhausts pointing to about 13ft. from the wagon. Behind the engines on the 'conflat' was a 325 gallon fuel tank, with a 24 volt battery system underneath the wagon. Behind the 'conflat' was another wagon carrying an 850 gallon road motor fuel tanker filled with jet fuel. At half power, snow was cleared virtually completely, and overall the tests were satisfactory, but somehow the scheme did not catch on (perhaps it was just too expensive).

Goods Yards and Docks

Plate 161: A view of Bristol (Temple Meads) goods station and yard alongside Temple Meads Station (extreme left) which is full of interest. The signal box in the centre was Temple Meads Goods Yard box, which opened in 1902 and was closed in 1970.

Plate 162: A scene of busy interchange of traffic between rail and barge. This particular view is of Brentford Dock in Middlesex. The two cranes shown are of varying lifting capacities, and the wharf was lit by the large wall lamps. The wooden platforms under the lamps could be fixed horizontally to allow the lamp men to service the gas lamps.

Accidents

Plates 163a, 163b & 163c: It is said that 'accidents do happen' and unfortunately the GWR had their share. The first two photographs show engine No. 1100, built at Swindon in January 1871 and involved in an accident at Norton Fitzwarren (which killed ten people) on 11th November 1890. It was repaired and continued in service until sold to the Government in 1916, and sent to Serbia to help the World War I effort. The broad gauge engine in the third picture, No. 2051, (built by Avonside Engine Co. in May 1873) was the other engine involved. This was in charge of a train from Plymouth Docks to Paddington, and ran into the stationary No. 1100. This engine was not repaired and these photographs were taken at Taunton in November 1890.

Plate 164: Another more minor mishap which was also recorded on film was this accident to 'Bulldog' class No. 3411 *Stanley Baldwin*, seen here with missing buffer beam and its front end distorted.

Weymouth and its Railway

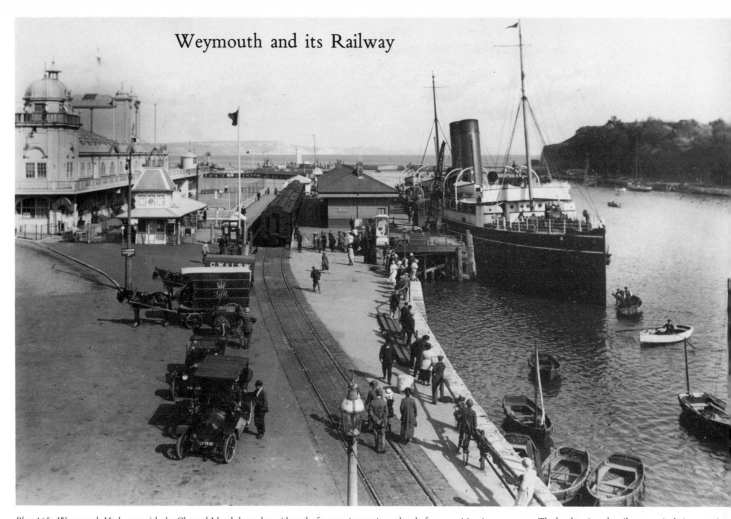

Plate 165: Weymouth Harbour, with the Channel Islands boat alongside and a four carriage train at the platform awaiting its passengers. The local taxis and mail cart await their respective loads, and many onlookers watch with interest. Note the GW&LSW Railways' parcels van. This view was photographed in the 1920s when the Quay Station had only one track, and only four carriages could be accommodated.

Plate 166: This shows the second platform line being installed on 13th April 1932 to handle the increased Channel Island traffic. The quay was extended, and platform accommodation was expanded so that no less than 36 coaches could now be accommodated. Freight had also increased, requiring the provision of a yard steam crane, as can be seen in the centre of the photograph.

Plates 167 & 168: Due to the sharp curves on the Weymouth Quay line, it was necessary to uncouple the screw couplings on passenger stock and replace them with special 3-link couplings. To avoid all this trouble and delay, the GWR, in 1938, carried out considerable improvements to the line, and these two pictures portray some of this work and show to what extent the Company valued the Channel Island revenue. Over 22,000 cub. yds. of rubble filling was used behind the new concrete quay wall, which was mostly brought in by rail.

Ships of the GWR

Plate 169: 'A floating craft of the Great Western Railway' was how the *GWR Magazine* described *SS The Mew*. The Dartmouth & Torbay Railway was authorised to run a ferry between Kingswear and Dartmouth. The first ferry, a paddle steamer, named *Dolphin*, was later acquired by the D&T Railway Co. (in 1873). After the GWR took over, *Dolphin* was replaced by *The Mew* on 31st May 1908, which was certified to carry 543 passengers, and this scene shows almost a capacity load. In 1939, it was recorded that *The Mew* made 23,000 trips across the River Dart, carried half a million passengers and 8,000 vehicles in the course of a year.

Plate 170 (above): The *Great Southern* was built in 1902 for the New Milford (Neyland) to Waterford service, later operated from Fishguard after the opening of that port. She was 275ft. long and 36ft. wide with a speed of 16 knots, and weighed 1,339 tons. Accommodating 680 passengers and 500 head of cattle, she crossed the St. George's Channel for 32 years, with occasional summer forays from Weymouth to the Channel Islands, until withdrawal in 1934.

Plate 171 (left): *St. Julien* made her maiden crossing between Weymouth and the Channel Islands on 23rd May 1925. She was one of four new steamers introduced by the GWR to their service (two for freight and two for passengers). Accommodation was for 1,000 passengers and she had a speed of 19 knots. This picture shows the steamer with only one funnel; when introduced she was a two funnel ship.

Freight Services

Plate 172: S.S. Pembroke lies alongside the jetty at Guernsey as the lorries and wagons arrive with tomatoes for loading and despatch to the mainland. The horse wagons, some already emptied, belong to the Fruit Export Co. Ltd.

Plate 173: The Great Western 'tender' *Sir Walter Raleigh* using a new adjustable electric conveyor to speed up the mail from boat to train in April 1927, at Plymouth Docks. The mail passed straight into the waiting GWR postal van, each van when full, being moved by a shunting engine.

Plate 174 (below): Cornish broccoli being loaded direct from farm to train at Penzance in April 1942. Note the wartime lorry headlights and white-faced wings.

Plate 175: Each year, with the advent of winter, the Witney Blanket Company despatched the results of its labour of the past twelve months. The output in 1923 was no less than 60,000 blankets, which were transported by the GWR to all parts of the country. This particular assignment with GWR 0-6-0PT No. 1249 in charge in Witney goods yard, is destined for Maple & Co. of London.

Plate 176: The view was typical of scenes at many stations in the 1920s, when the milk traffic carried by the Great Western was enormous. Although published before, this photograph, taken at Highbridge Station in Somerset on 2nd February 1928, shows a line up of Albion lorries of the Wilts United Dairy Co. together with empty milk churns.

Plate 177: Birkenhead goods shed (Morpeth Dock) on 5th March 1924. The interest here lies in the fact that the wharf and barges are situated between the lines of wagons, and can be seen in the middle left of the photograph; this allowed direct loading from rail to water (barges). A very hectic scene has been captured here by the staff photographer.

Plate 178: Christmas mail at Paddington in 1926. With the Royal Mail van standing by, and the bags all ready sorted into areas such as 'Eastern', 'Western', etc., the staff get ready to load. The watchful eye of the law looks on.

Plate 179: The Great Western were renowned for their participation in shows and exhibitions, and not only did they transport exhibits for companies, but also used their vehicles as examples of loading and unloading equipment. On 27th May 1930, deliveries are being made to the Bath & West and Southern Counties Show at Torquay, and this shows a portable crane unloading at Torre. The lorry is an AEC 3½ ton with a flat body, No. 286, converted in 1927. Again this photograph was used for publicity purposes.

Plate 180 (below): This Engineering Department wagon had the telegraphic code name of 'GANE', and was one of twenty one constructed in the 1900s. This particular bogie vehicle was converted to carry cast-iron pipes from the Staveley Coal & Iron Co. of Chesterfield, to Swindon Works for the new gas plant and associated pipe lines at the Works.

DOOR TO DOOR CONVEYANCE

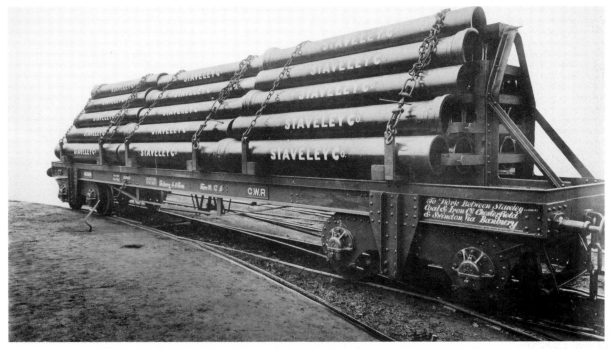

Plate 181: Under the heading 'Freight Services', this view shows a demonstration of the incredible amount of traffic once handled in South Wales. How many loaded wagons can be seen in this photograph taken in 1906 of Swansea Docks and transfer sidings? The docks, ships and cranes can be seen in the background on the right.

Freight Wagons

Plate 182 (below): Photographed on 25th August 1936 at Morris Cowley, Oxford, for publicity purposes, this shows how the transportation of new Morris cars was carried out by the GWR. This particular picture was taken to record the method of securing the front of the motor car in the 'Mogo' covered motor car truck, No. 105708. These wagons had special end doors which, when opened, and when the space between the vans were bridged with small ramps, enabled the cars to be driven right through the train, resulting in very quick loading. Night-time loading was achieved with the help of the car head-lights.

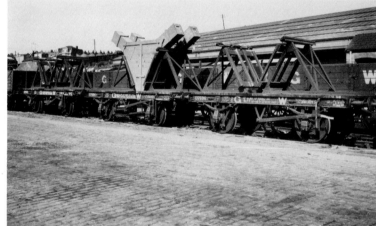

Plate 183: During World War II, wagons had to be converted in a hurry to suit special traffic. One such conversion was for the transportation of the aeroplane propeller, and here we see 'ROLL' wagons so converted to carry Wellington propellers (two per wagon). After the war, the wagons reverted to their original uses.

Plate 184: Ship propellers were also carried and here again these were bulky and heavy objects, so the GWR used their 'CROCODILE F' trolley wagons for the duty. The all-up weight carried was 25 tons, evenly distributed. The way the wagon is loaded is worth studying, and also note how the photographic department has tried to remove the gentleman in the bottom left corner of the picture by retouching the negative.

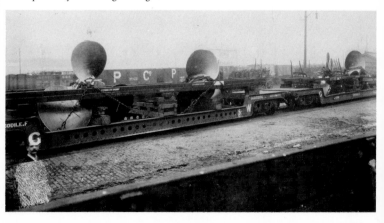

Plate 185: An insulated container on a flat wagon ('SERPENT C') is shown at Paddington goods yard on 19th June 1930. This container was designed for a 4 ton load of meat, and was painted white with red lettering. Again the GWR were pioneers in this type of freight handling. Note the 'instanter' type of coupling; the middle link of this 3-link coupling could be turned so that the other two links were brought closer together, thus shortening the coupling. This reduced the recoil of wagons when stopping or starting, minimising the possibility of damage to their contents.

Loads

Plate 186 (above): Fishguard on 22nd July 1930. A motor car being loaded on to the *SS St. Andrew*. The photograph was taken to record the method of loading such a cargo.

Plate 187: One of the Ransome 1 ton mobile cranes at work at Westbourne Park, London, on 16th January 1928 and photographed to demonstrate the flexibility and ease of handling of container traffic. This particular crane was later fitted with a protection frame above the driver's head to avoid the jib coming down too far and causing personal injury.

Plate 188: A street in Acton photographed on 11th November 1930, showing the new company housing.

The GWR thought highly of their staff, and in the 1930s built attractive houses for them in many areas. The distribution of the houses throughout the system was as follows:

London (Acton)	762
Severn Tunnel Junction	42
Plymouth	164
Truro	36
Caerphilly	58
Penzance	20
Swansea	107
Barry	108
Exeter	32

Plate 189: This illustrates a rather hilly estate in Laira, Plymouth, on 8th November 1930.

The Acton estate in London was called the London Garden Village Society and also incorporated shops adjoining West Acton Station. The London Society was the largest of the housing societies, and was managed entirely by the GWR staff themselves. Several of the estates also had a reading room and a library. These communities managed to produce plays, concerts, bazaars and a debating society.

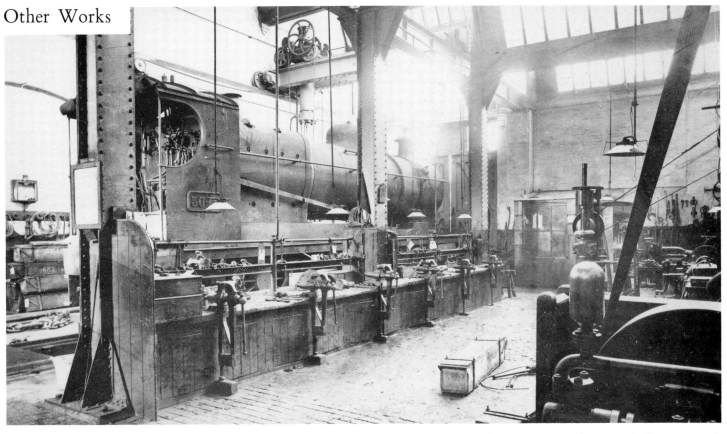

Plate 190: With such a large area to cover, the GWR built workshops and facilities around the whole system, and the lifting shop at Exeter is shown on 18th February 1936, with GWR 'R.O.D.' class No. 3045 being repaired.

Plate 191: The works at Caerphilly (seven miles from Cardiff) were inherited from the Rhymney Railway Co. under the Railways Act of 1921. Although chiefly a locomotive repair works, it was decided, in late 1936, to establish a carriage repair shop there, and a new building was constructed alongside the old carriage & wagon shop. It comprised two bays, each 424ft. long. The new overhead travelling cranes of 20 tons capacity were specially designed with grabs and made lifting coach bodies look easy. Photographed in December 1939 lifting a body clear of bogies, these cranes could also move sideways over the tracks.

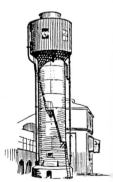

Water Softener

Plate 192: Tyseley Erecting Shop in December 1910, with at least seven locomotives in various stages of major repair. This view shows that mainly the smaller classes of engines from the Birmingham Division were handled here.

Plate 193: In 1920, the Great Western Railway constructed a garage workshop at Alfred Road, Westbourne Park in West London to service their growing fleet of road vehicles. Consisting of three servicing bays, stores and machine shop, with separate offices and messrooms, it was a great improvement on the previous facilities. This view was photographed on 10th July 1934 and shows a considerable range of vehicles in various states of repair.

The majesty, design and finish of Great Western locomotives was, I feel, of the highest quality, and the Company never missed recording the introduction of a new class or change in livery, so this section commences with three pictures from the vast Swindon locomotive photograph collection.

Plate 194: Firstly we see the largest engine on any railway in 1908, No. 111 *The Great Bear*, a 4-6-2 Pacific built at Swindon Works during that year. This particular picture was taken in 1917 after its final refurbishment at Swindon Works; it was scrapped in 1924. It is recorded that it was a bad steamer and its duties were mainly on minor expresses and night freight duties between Paddington and Bristol. Although the front of the engine and the boiler gives an impression of great power, from the firebox backwards, I feel the design aesthetically just did not 'come off' — look at that tiny cab!

Plate 195 (right): At the other end of the scale this view shows a new 0-4-0T dock locomotive ordered for Swansea Docks, and constructed by the Avonside Engine Company in 1926 to a GWR design, but painted at Swindon Works in the Company's livery and duly photographed for the record book.

Plate 196 (below): The last look at the official posed locomotive showing a complete side view of a 2021 class 0-6-0PT, No. 2151.

Plate 197: Obviously many exciting and interesting events happened at Swindon, and the official photographer was always on hand to capture the moment. One such event, in 1924, was the testing ordered by C. B. Collett (Chief Mechanical Engineer) of a new 'Castle' class engine No. 4074 *Caldicot Castle*, the second 'Castle' to be built, which made three trial runs from Swindon to Plymouth and back. The loads on the 'down' runs were fourteen heavy 70ft. eight-wheeled coaches and a dynamometer car (from Swindon to Taunton), eleven coaches from Taunton to Newton Abbot, and eight coaches from Newton Abbot to Plymouth. Times were scheduled to equal the fastest expresses running over that part of the system. The tests carried out were very comprehensive indeed.

Plate 198: This shows how some of the inspectors had to travel and work.

Plate 199: The actual dynamometer car used in the tests is shown here. More than seventeen individual tests were carried out on the 'Castle' class trials, and these are listed below:

Measurements and records were made of the following:

(1) Indicates horse-power.
(2) Pressure in the steam chest.
(3) Drawbar pull and drawbar horse-power.
(4) Speed.

(5) Steam pressure, cut off, opening of regulator, and height of water in gauge glass.
(6) Coal consumed.
(7) Water consumed.
(8) Oil consumed.
(9) Vacuum in the smokebox and pressure in the ashpan.
(10) Temperature of the feed water in the tender.
(11) Temperature of the feed water entering the boiler.
(12) Pressure of the exhaust steam entering the exhaust steam injector.
(13) Temperature of:
    (a) Superheater flues.
    (b) Steam entering the superheater.
    (c) Steam leaving the superheater.
    (d) Steam entering the steam chest.
    (e) Smokebox generally.
(14) The chemical composition of:
    (a) Smokebox gases.
    (b) Coal (also the calorific value).
    (c) Smokebox ashes.
    (d) Ashes in the ashpan.
(15) Weight of the smokebox ashes.
(16) Weight of the ashpan ashes.
(17) Wind and weather.

Plates 200a & 200b: With the Automatic Train Control system proving its reliability on the main line between Paddington and Reading for over twenty five years, the Company decided, in 1930, to vastly extend the system from 372 track miles to 2,130 track miles. This meant a further 2,000 locomotives had to be equipped with ATC and these two photographs were taken to record the ramp shoe at the rear of the locomotive and the apparatus in the cab (the box with bell above, adjacent to the right-hand window).

Plate 201: It was found that the fitting of the ATC shoe at the rear of the locomotive was not entirely successful, because if the locomotive bounced whilst travelling at speed, the shoe could miss the ramp altogether. Later, therefore, it was repositioned at the front of the locomotive and this photograph was taken to record this change.

Plate 200a

Plate 200b

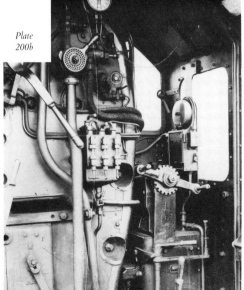

Plate 202: Oil burning engines were introduced in 1946, with a 'Hall' class 4-6-0 locomotive, No. 5955 *Garth Hall* being the first to be converted from burning coal to burning oil. The tender was fitted with a large fuel tank which allowed the 'Hall' to travel up to 250 miles between refuelling. This obviously meant the facility of oil refuelling at many major depots, and this view of the oil refuelling plant at Swindon in 1947 shows converted 'Castle' No. 5083 *Bath Abbey* in the process of replenishment. This engine was oil-fired from 6th December 1946 to 4th November 1948.

Plate 203: Whenever the GWR had the opportunity to run a special, they tried to arrange a smokebox door headboard to advertise the fact, and here at Old Oak Common, 'Star' class 4-6-0 No. 4022 *King William* poses for the 'official record'. This engine was built in July 1909 at a cost of £3,102, ran over two million miles, and was renamed *The Belgian Monarch* in 1927. Its name was slightly altered by the removal of *'The'* in November 1927, but the nameplate was removed in May 1940, because of the war situation. No. 4022 was cut up in 1952 (see *Plate 28* illustrating this locomotive under repair in Swindon Works).

Plate 204: Running through Swindon centre road, in September 1933, is 2-8-0 28XX class No. 2808 with a long freight. The reason for this photograph is again not obvious, and the records do not give the answer.

Plate 205: These water troughs between Pangbourne and Goring were 620yds. long and were one of only fourteen sets of troughs on the GWR system. The only other troughs installed on quadruple track were between Cogload and Creech Junction in Somerset. The water tank which maintained the level of water is seen on the extreme right. The water was taken from the River Thames but was passed through an elaborate water softening plant, thus reducing the 'scaling', from hard water, in the engine boilers.

Plate 206: The Railway Centenary celebrations were held at Darlington in July 1925, and on 2nd July the great procession took place. The Great Western was well represented and a full scale model of *North Star* (originally built in 1837) was the first to trundle along, followed by three other GWR exhibits; No. 4700, a 2-8-0 built in 1919; No,. 5225, a 2-8-0 side tank mineral engine for use in the Welsh Valleys; and No. 4082 *Windsor Castle* (seen here), a 4-6-0 hauling an immaculate Royal Train. Note the refreshment table, with waitress, near the line-side. The small plaque above the number of engine No. 4082 has the inscription *(below)* engraved upon it.

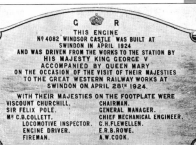

G R
THIS ENGINE
Nº 4082 WINDSOR CASTLE WAS BUILT AT
SWINDON IN APRIL 1924
AND WAS DRIVEN FROM THE WORKS TO THE STATION BY
HIS MAJESTY KING GEORGE V
ACCOMPANIED BY QUEEN MARY
ON THE OCCASION OF THE VISIT OF THEIR MAJESTIES
TO THE GREAT WESTERN RAILWAY WORKS AT
SWINDON ON APRIL 28TH 1924.

WITH THEIR MAJESTIES ON THE FOOTPLATE WERE
VISCOUNT CHURCHILL.   CHAIRMAN.
SIR FELIX POLE.   GENERAL MANAGER.
MR C.B.COLLETT.   CHIEF MECHANICAL ENGINEER.
    LOCOMOTIVE INSPECTOR.   C.H.FLEWELLEN.
    ENGINE DRIVER.   E.R.B.ROWE.
    FIREMAN.   A.W.COOK.

Plate 207 (above): The last GWR engine in the Railway Centenary celebrations was 4-6-0 'Castle' No. 111 *Viscount Churchill* drawing the new articulated coaching stock. This engine was rebuilt in 1924 from *The Great Bear*, 4-6-2 Pacific (see *Plate 194*) and was used on express services between Paddington and Plymouth.

Plate 208 (below): A special train called 'The Girder Special' left Chepstow at 1.20p.m. on 15th April 1931. 'Dean Goods' 0-6-0 No. 2465 is seen moving one of the seven 32 ton girders. No. 2465 was built in 1896 and was withdrawn in 1940.

20 Ton Wagon

Plate 209: One of the biggest changes to the freight scene was the new 20 ton mineral wagons introduced in 1924 to increase payloads and reduce the number of wagons required. This particular wagon was one of over 1,300 new all-metal wagons built under Diagram No. N23 in 1924/5 with end tipping and one side door, for North's Navigation Collieries. These wagons were soon to become increasingly abundant throughout the system.

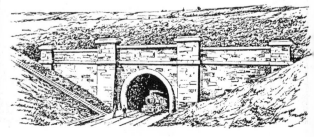

Plate 210: Photographed at Swindon Carriage Works on 20th January 1934, a 31ft. camp coach, No. 9988, (with a single sweep roof) stands resplendent in chocolate and cream livery. Great Western carriages were painted brown all over until October 1864, when the Directors' decided that the tops of the carriages of all classes should, in future, be painted white. When varnished, this produced the familiar cream tint. Cream and brown remained the standard for all passenger coaches until 1909, except for one train, which was painted dark lake, experimentally, in 1903. Brown, all over, was then resumed, to be changed to crimson lake in 1912. This lasted for ten years, after which brown (popularly known as chocolate) and cream were once more made the standard colours.

Plate 211: Special saloon No. 9006 which is featured here, although ordered and built in 1944, was not put into service until 1945. Built on an old underframe, No. 9006 had a sleeping compartment for train staff, a kitchen, an eight seat dining room, a bathroom, two bedrooms and a full width saloon. In 1948, No. 9006 was incorporated into the new Royal Train, and air conditioning was installed. This Swindon Carriage Works photograph was taken on 10th November 1944 just after completion.

Plate 212: This Royal carriage was the first eight-wheeled coach to be built at Swindon Works for the standard gauge. The vehicle, as can be seen, had a large bulge in the middle to allow for the wider and higher main saloon. The oil lamps in the roof were rather larger than usual, especially over the saloon area. The splendid painting and lining of the vehicle is clearly visible in this fine official photograph.

Plate 213: This photograph was taken on 10th February 1928 as supporting evidence in an accident case within the Company. The official photographers were often called upon to record these mishaps. The large brackets midway up the vehicles are to carry side lights if forming the last vehicle of a train. The use of side lights on passenger trains was not abolished until 1st June 1933. Luckily these 'routine' photographs now reveal small details useful to the railway enthusiast.

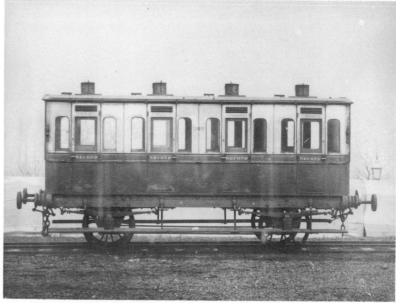

Plate 214: A very early 1880s official photograph illustrates a second class four-wheeled carriage, No. 385. Note the white sheets behind the vehicle to blank out the background. Each of the four doors is numbered 385J, 385K, 385M and 385N, respectively, identifying each compartment. Note there was no lettering or Company monogram at this time.

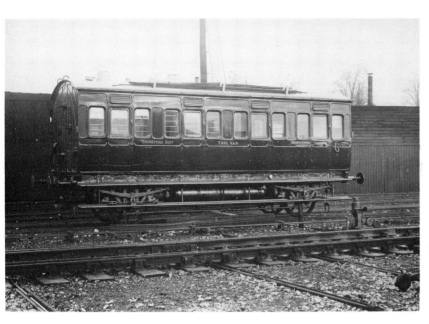

Plate 215: A four-wheeled carriage (originally constructed before the turn of the century) converted into an Engineering Department tool van No. 14935. Having just been completed, the official photographer has been called in to 'capture' the smart vehicle on film.

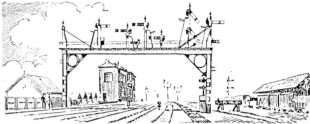

Signalling

Plate 216: Reading West Junction and the fine array of early GWR signals are well defined. The line to Oxford Road Junction, and the West Country, curves off to the right in advance of the signal box. The signals show the early use of red for 'danger' and a clear white for 'all clear'; a green spectacle replaced the white indication from January 1895 onwards.

Plate 217: Many interior photographs were taken of signal boxes and this is a 1903 view of Reading Main Line West box. This box was 105ft. long and contained a 185 lever frame (after 1912 this was expanded to 222 levers including spaces and was the largest mechanical box on the system). The box was worked by three signalmen, one of whom would have been in charge, and a booking boy (on the left). With the long block shelf across the windows, the signalmen's view of operations would have been very limited, and there was no illuminated diagram in those days to assist their control of movements.

Plate 218: An unusual signal box, to say the least! Photographed in the early 1900s, Bristol East Depot No. 2 signal box is situated half-way up the cliff face. This was built in this position as there just was not enough room for the box to be alongside the track. Note the protection covering over the stairway against falling rocks, and how the whole box is supported on four girders horizontally out from the rock face.

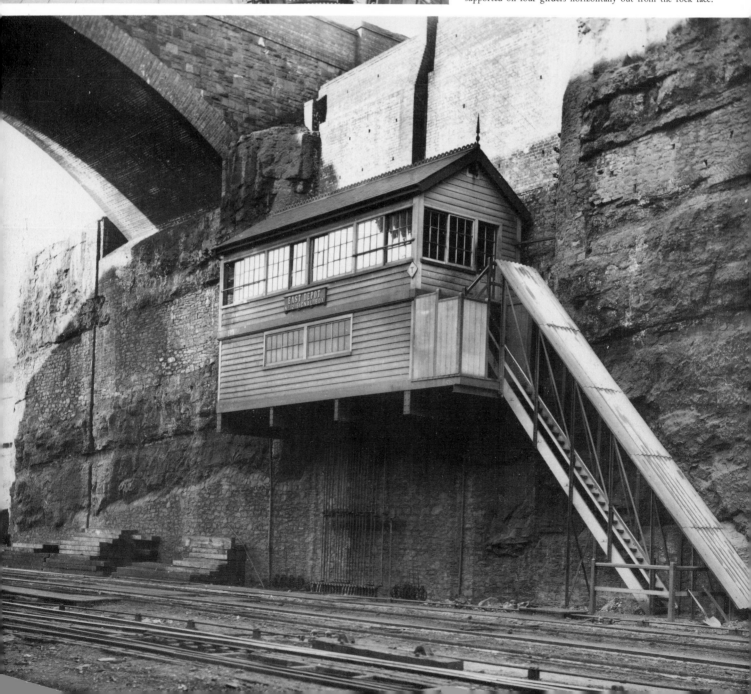

Plate 219: This photograph was taken as part of the record of the widening between Olton and Lapworth. Bentley Heath Crossing signal box (new in 1932) and very wide crossing gates, plus new telegraph posts and footbridge, are clearly visible in this May 1934 photograph.

Plate 220: Gaer Junction signal box on the main line just west of Newport. Behind the cameraman is Newport Tunnel, and this photograph was possibly taken in 1912 when the line was quadrupled between Newport Station and Alexandra Dock Junction, involving a new double line tunnel and new signal box at Gaer Junction. The double line on the extreme right of the picture leads through Gaer Tunnel (403yds.) to Park Junction (on the Western Valley section), whilst just above the third telegraph pole in the line of poles (on the left of the picture) is Maesglas Junction signal box, also on the Western Valley line which crosses the main line by a bridge at this point. Note that the double junctions in front of the signal box are clamped for straight running.

Plate 221: A fine study of Bishton Crossing signal box between Severn Tunnel Junction and Newport, in 1910 obviously photographed not long after completion as everything is new, including the crossing gates. A well detailed picture.

Plate 222: Built in 1891, this signal box at Goring & Streatley features an unusual style of brick and wood structure, with a narrow base, because of the restricted site between the main and relief lines. This view shows the 49 lever box (the second one at Goring), which was extended in 1960 to hold 65 levers; it closed on 9th May 1965. The garden and newly-planted bushes on the left, outlined in whitewashed stones, were obviously the signalman's pride and joy.

Plate 223: Bristol (Temple Meads) East box was one of three power signal boxes built in 1935 to replace five existing manual boxes at Bristol. These new boxes broke away from standard GWR construction techniques and were steel-framed with brick walls. The upper floor at East box was for signal operation, the middle floor held the electrical relays, and the ground floor accommodated the workshop, linesmen stores, and cable room. East box had a frame containing 368 miniature levers and 18 push buttons working 'calling-on' signals. The old signal gantry can still be seen on the right, prior to being dismantled. This box was eventually replaced in 1971.

Plate 224: For use at Bristol, the GWR installed searchlight signals (seen here). The gantries and brackets were supplied by the Reading Signal Works, whereas the signal contractor supplied the tubular masts and fittings. This type of signal was used on the approaches to Bristol, whilst multiple lens signals were sited in the station area.

Plate 225: The Westland Wessex aircraft of 1933, a six seater aeroplane which initiated the GWR Cardiff to South Devon service was provided, together with crew, by Imperial Airways.

Air Services

Plate 226a: On 15th May 1933, the air service was introduced from Birmingham to Cardiff and Haldon (for Teignmouth and Torquay), and then on to Plymouth. This was a daily flight each way, including Sundays. This poster advertises this service.

Plate 226b: The route which applied from 12th April 1933, which did not incl Birmingham, is shown in this smaller poster.

AIR SERVICES
BIRMINGHAM
CARDIFF
TEIGNMOUTH
TORQUAY
PLYMOUTH

GREAT WESTERN RAILWAY
AIR SERVICES

Commencing April 12th, 1933, the Great Western Railway Company will inaugurate an Air Service between

PLYMOUTH (Plymouth Air Port)
TORQUAY & TEIGNMOUTH
Haldon Aerodrome
and **CARDIFF** (Air Port)

FLYING TIME

From Plymouth Air Port	From Haldon Aerodrome
75 Minutes	50 Minutes

Imperial Airways Westland Wessex
6-Seater 3-Engined Air Liner & Pilot

HEAVY LUGGAGE COLLECTED, CONVEYED BY RAIL AND DELIVERED WITHOUT EXTRA CHARGE

Special bus services connecting Stations and Aerodromes

FARES to CARDIFF	FROM	Single	Return
	PLYMOUTH AIR PORT AND BUS FROM PLYMOUTH, MILLBAY STATION	£3-10	£6
	HALDON AERODROME AND BUS FROM TEIGNMOUTH AND TORQUAY	£3	£5

G.W.R. AIR MAIL 3D

Plate 227: A further view of a different aircraft used on the air service, but with the Company crest on the tail. The lettering on the fuselage reads GREAT WESTERN AIR SERVICES, and it was reported that this aeroplane was in the chocolate and cream livery.

Plate 228: Later in the 1930s, as the service became more widely used, larger aeroplanes were operated, and the Dragon Rapide DH84 biplane, seen here, was pressed into service, with the Railway Air Services covering the whole of Britain. This included limited freight, and Richmond Sausages seem to be the 'freight of the day'.

Plate 229: This photograph illustrates the refuelling of these aeroplanes in those early aviation days, once again recorded by an official photographer.

Paddington Station

Plate 230 (left lower): Holiday crowds in July 1912 pack the wooden platforms of Paddington Station. Note the side lamps on the rear of the trains on platform 2 and 3 (*see Plate 213*).

Plate 231: Platform 1 at Paddington, prior to World War I. The new route via Princes Risborough (Leamington in 1hr. 31mins) is announced on one of the numerous posters on the walls. Carriage pilot No. 8 has just pulled in a set of coaching stock, the rear vehicle being a clerestory slip coach, with the vacuum reservoir tanks along the whole length of the roof.

The staff magazine challenged the public to suggest the origination of the station name Paddington, and five of the answers make interesting reading. Perhaps, now, further suggestions will be forthcoming.

Dear Sir — Your correspondent is slightly inaccurate in assuming that the 'ton' in Paddington means 'town'; its original signification was that of the earthen mound which was thrown up round a settlement for purposes of defence. The rest of the name indicates that the township originated in a settlement of a family of freemen, i.e. the Paddings, the tribe or family of the 'Padds'. The word is thus distinguished from words such as 'Clapham' or 'Alfreton', where the name of a man followed by the suffix -ton or -ham, suggest that the township started from a nucleus composed of the dependents of one of the great chiefs and was the township of the people of Clapa or Alfred.

Yours faithfully,
MABEL G. HINTON.

Dear Sir — I think the following is a possible explanation: The old English suffix 'ing', meant 'sons of'. It is probable that originally a man by the name of 'Padd' settled in this particular spot of London and had sons who were called 'Padding', the locality being eventually named Paddington — the town of the 'Padding'. We have the same sort of thing in the word, Nott-ing-ham: 'ham' of course meaning 'home'.

Yours truly;
A. E. CREEDY

Sir — Pad-ing-ton: the other *d* is an odd one put in. *Pad* — an old word for *path*; *ing* — a noun ending; *ton* — town. Thus Paddington is *pathtown*, or the *town on the path*. *Pad* for *path* is still heard in country places where the English tongue is spoken. *Foot-pad* is well-known. Then it was made to become the name of the robber lurking in the hedge to spoil the wayfarer.

C. J. WISE

The Deputy Town Clerk at Paddington supplies the following extract from the Preface of *Paddington, Past and Present* by William Robins. 'Mr. B. H. Smart, the well-known English scholar, kindly suggested to me some time since, the possibility of the word 'Paddington' being derived from 'Padre-ing-tun' — the father's 'town meadow', and Sir Harry Dene Goring, of Bayswater House, was so good as to suggest another derivation which, I think, it is right to acknowledge in this place. In a note Sir Harry writes me on this subject, he says: 'A 'pad' is a Sussex word now in common use for pack-horse- 'ings' we have in that county by the hundreds'. Now the carriers to the great city may have lodged and had meadows for their pack-horses here. I humbly suggest, therefore, may not Paddington mean 'the village of the pack horse meadows?'

The following is another extract from the same book: 'The fact of Paddington, in Surrey, or 'Padendene', as it was called, being mentioned in the Conqueror's survey, while Paddington, in Middlesex, was not noticed, inclines me to believe the *dene* or *den*, in Surrey, was the original mark of the Poedings; and that the smaller enclosure in Middlesex was at first peopled and cultivated by a migration of a portion of that family from the *den*, when it had become inconveniently full'.

Plate 232 (above): A packed Armistice Day memorial service on No. 1 platform at Paddington Station, taking place on 11th November 1926. The General Manager of the Great Western Railway, Sir Felix Pole, is standing on the clergyman's left, with James Milne, the Assistant General Manager, on his left. The gentleman with white beard and moustache (three away from Sir Felix Pole) is Mr R. H. Nicholls, Superintendent of the line. Similar scenes took place at many other stations, works and depots within the system.

Plate 233: The 'corridors of power' at Paddington Station (first floor, eastern end). Many relics, photographs and paintings hang in these corridors which overlooked No. 1 platform. Notice the timber model viaduct on the right and the slotted post signals. The light above the steps is the balcony window overlooking the whole of Paddington Station. This balcony can be seen in *Plate 232* at the top left of the photograph.

Miscellaneous

Plate 234: A remarkable log arrived at Swindon Works in November 1923 and is 'officially photographed' alongside a 12 ton open wagon for length comparison. The log was of Polish oak, shipped from Danzig, and measured 44ft. long by 26in. in diameter, and contained 164 cub. ft. of timber. This was recorded as the best oak log ever received at Swindon Works. The GWR seemed reluctant to use it, as the photograph is dated 28th February 1924!

Plate 235: Under the heading 'Accidents that are asked for' an article in the staff magazine was accompanied by this photograph, and continued:

'There are risks inseparable from every calling. It's a pity, but there it is. Of course, sensible men try to avoid them. Self-preservation is a natural instinct. There might be excuses for lack of foresight or want of thought, but what shall we say of men who, in cold blood, actually adopt dangerous and forbidden practices for so small a purpose as saving themselves a few yards' walk? Look at this picture. Probably there are few readers to whom the sight is unfamiliar. What does that mean? It means that the practice of riding on a shunting-pole is a common one. Everyone knows that it is forbidden. And why? Obviously because of its danger. Many an unfortunate fellow has attempted it to his peril. There is a man at Paddington who, nineteen years ago, lost both his legs through doing this. A sudden jerk of the vehicles threw him off the shunting pole, which caught him in the back and knocked him down, and his legs were run over. A thoughtless moment entailed disablement for the rest of his life. Scores of other serious accidents have happened in the same way'.

Many official photographs like this were taken to be used in 'Safety Movement' pamphlets and booklets, issued by the GWR.

Plate 236: This photograph of Silverton Station was taken purely for an early article in the *GWR Magazine*, relating that the stationmaster had constructed an observatory in his garden and spent all his off-duty hours stargazing. Such was the diversity of the staff photographer's subjects.

Plate 237: The photographers were also called upon to record objects, plans and correspondence, and one such item was a letter to Chief Constable Wilson, of Cardiff, on 28th June 1927, with details of a suspected planned mail bag robbery and was signed, 'Poorly paid labourer'.

Plate 238: On 6th April 1935, a scene portraying the arrival at Maidenhead of a train on the day of the opening of the railway between London and Maidenhead, was re-enacted for a GWR film. The actors, mainly Company employees who were members of the operatic societies, were highly commended on their performances in the making of the centenary film. A 'still' from the film for the GWR files is seen here.

TO STOP THE TRAIN IN CASE
OF EMERGENCY
PULL DOWN THE CHAIN
PENALTY FOR IMPROPER USE £5

Plate 239: The arrival of the GWR Magazine each month at Paddington created a considerable amount of extra work, and here the porters are 'mustering' for the mammoth unloading session and redistribution to all parts of the system. The magazine was the most important periodical that the Company produced, and not only recorded engineering achievements but family events, staff promotions, etc. A form of insurance against personal injury was given to every member of the staff who purchased a copy.

Plate 241 (below): The presentation of a superb grandfather clock to Mr William Dean (Locomotive & Carriage Superintendent and Superintendent of Swindon Works) on his retirement in 1901, warranted an official photograph and this was the result. Mr. Dean remarked at the presentation that 'it was a renewal of a reminder from his early days of apprenticeship of the necessity of good timekeeping'.

Plate 240: Photographed on 14th February 1911, and recorded as 'Lamp versus Partridge', this picture is another oddity in the official collection, but obviously worthy of a 12in. x 10in. plate glass negative.

Plate 242: A blackbird's nest was found in the underframe of a scrapped wagon in May 1926. A final 'fun' picture from the camera of the official GWR photographer. These men had to travel many miles and brave inclement weather to carry out their tasks, and compile a record for posterity of one of the finest railway companies Great Britain has ever known. No wonder it was nicknamed 'God's Wonderful Railway'.

Some Early Dates

SOME INTERESTING DATES IN THE HISTORY OF THE GREAT WESTERN RAILWAY COMPANY UP TO THE GROUPING

1833,	JULY	30	Public meeting held at Bristol to promote a railway from Bristol to London.
	AUG.	19	First Meeting of Board of Management of the Company. Title of "Great Western Railway" recorded for the first time.
1833,			First Prospectus of G.W.R. issued.
1835,	AUG.	31	Great Western Railway Act received Royal Assent
1838,	JUNE	4	G.W.R. opened from Paddington to Maidenhead Bridge.
1839,			Electric Telegraph installed on line from Paddington to West Drayton.
1840,	MAR.	30	G.W.R. extended to Reading.
	JUNE	1	G.W.R. extended to Steventon.
	JULY	20	G.W.R. extended to Faringdon Road.
	AUG.	31	G.W.R. extended to opened from Bristol to Bath.
	DEC.	16	G.W.R. extended to Wootton Bassett.
	DEC.	16	First portion of Taff Vale Railway opened.
1841,	MAY	31	G.W.R. extended to Chippenham
	JUNE	30	G.W.R. extended to Bath.
	AUG.	31	G.W.R. opened throughout to Bristol.
	JUNE	14	First portion of Bristol & Exeter Railway opened.
			Didcot to Oxford Branch opened.
1842,	JUNE	13	Queen Victoria made her first railway journey, on G.W.R.
	SEPT.	29	First excursion train from Bristol to London.
1843,			Swindon-Gloucester line amalgamated with G.W.R.
1844,			Didcot-Oxford branch amalgamated with G.W.R.
1846,			Exeter-Newton Abbot section of S. Devon Railway opened. Cloak rooms for passengers' luggage inaugurated. Cardboard tickets adopted by G.W.R.
1847,			Gloucester-Cheltenham Railway opened. Reading-Hungerford branch opened. Atmospheric system came into operation on S. Devon Railway.
1848,			Shrewsbury and Chester railway opened. S. Devon Railway opened to Plymouth and Torquay.
1849,	OCT.	8	Windsor branch opened.
1850,			Chepstow-Swansea section of S. Wales Railway opened.
1851,	JULY	1	Kennet and Avon Canal purchased by G.W.R. Chepstow-Grange Court section of S. Wales Railway opened.
1852,			West Cornwall Railway opened.
	JULY	14	Chepstow Bridge completed. Route from London to S. Wales opened. Oxford-Birmingham line opened.
1853,			Hereford and Ludlow line opened.
1854,	JAN	17	New Station at Paddington opened. Maidenhead-High Wycombe branch opened. Shrewsbury and Chester, and Shrewsbury and Birmingham Railways amalgamated with G.W.R.
1856,			S. Wales Railway extended to New Milford.
1857,			Henley branch opened. Channel Islands steamboat service from Weymouth began.
1859,	MAY	2	Saltash Bridge opened. Cornwall Railway opened.
	SEPT.	15	Isambard Kingdom Brunel died.
1860,			First broad-gauge train ran from Paddington to Penzance. First interlocked signal frame used on G.W.R.
1862,			"Flying Dutchman" put on.
1863,	JAN.	10	Metropolitan Railway opened, and worked by G.W.R.
	AUG.	1	West Midland and S. Wales Railways amalgamated with G.W.R.
		24	Falmouth branch of Cornwall Railway opened. Spagnoletti block signal instruments introduced.
1864,			Mr. D. Gooch resigned post of Locomotive Superintendent. Hammersmith and City Railway opened.
1865,			Shrewsbury and Welshpool Railway amalgamated with G.W.R. and L.& N.W.R. jointly. Sir. D. Gooch elected Chairman of G.W.R.
1869,			Broad gauge removed from Metropolitan Railway. Hereford, Ross and Gloucester Railway converted to narrow gauge.
1871,			"Caution" position of signals discontinued on G.W.R.
1872,			Severn Tunnel Act passed. South Wales Railway converted to narrow gauge.
1873,			Shah of Persia received at Paddington.
1874,			Quadrupling of G.W.R. tracks from London-Didcot begun.
1875,			Vacuum brake adopted by G.W.R.
1876,			West Cornwall and Bristol & Exeter Railways amalgamated with G.W.R.
1877,			Bala and Dolgelley Railway amalgamated with G.W.R.
1878,			South Devon Railway amalgamated with G.W.R. Subway for Hammersmith and City Railway between Paddington and Westbourne Park opened.
1879,			Severn Bridge opened. Iron wagon frames introduced on G.W.R.
1880,			Paddington Station lighted by electricity.
1881,			Headings of Severn Tunnel met.
1882,			Third-class on all G.W.R. passenger trains except certain expresses.
1886,	JAN.	9	First goods train ran through Severn Tunnel.
	DEC.	1	First passenger train ran through Severn Tunnel.
1888,			"Great Western Railway Magazine" started.
1890,			First corridor train on G.W.R.
	OCT.	1	Third-class on all G.W.R. passenger trains.
1893,			Steam heating of trains introduced on G.W.R.
1895,			Compulsory ten minute stop at Swindon abolished. Water-troughs laid on G.W.R. tracks. Bath and Bristol services accelerated.
1896,			First-class dining cars started. Paddington Station Hotel reverted to G.W.R. control.
	OCT.	13	Fast service to Devon and Cornwall announced.
1899,			Non-stop London-Exeter and London-Birmingham trains put on.
1901,	JULY	1	Stert-Westbury "cut-off" opened. Third-class saloons introduced. Chain communication inside carriages adopted.
1903,	JULY	1	South Wales Direct route opened for passenger trains.
	AUG.	3	First G.W.R. motor-bus put into service. Rail motor-cars introduced. Third-class dining-cars on expresses.
1904,	JULY	1	London-Plymouth non-stop express put on.
1905,			Incadescent gas lighting of carriages introduced. First power signalling equipment installed (Didcot).
1906,	JAN	1	Audible signalling on locomotives tried.
1906,	JUNE	29	Castle Cary-Langport "cut-off" opened.
	JULY		"Cornish Riviera Express" inaugurated.
	AUG.	30	Fishguard-Rosslare service began.
1908,			"Pacific" locomotive, "Great Bear," put into service.
1910,			Ashenden-Aynho "cut-off," and short route to Birmingham opened.
	OCT.	1	Second-class abolished on G.W.R.
1914,	AUG.	4	G.W.R. taken over by Government.
1915,	FEB.	1	G.W.R. district raided by Zeppelins.
1920,	AUG.	3	Ealing and Shepherd's Bush Railway opened.
1921,	AUG.	15	Government control ceased.
	OCT.	3	Through service between Aberdeen and Penzance inaugurated.
1923,	JAN.	1	Great Western Group began to function.